CONTENTS

CHAPTER 1: INTRODUCING THE POWER XL SMOKELESS ELECTRIC GRILL

Do you love to enjoy succulent and juicy grilled steaks and chops? But hate to set up a charcoal grill just because it's messy? Do you want an indoor grill that will not cook without smoke but also give charcoal grill like flavors to your food? Well, try the new Power XL smokeless electric grill! This electric grill literally sucks back the smoke back in and keep your kitchen environment 100 percent smoke-free. Charcoal or gas grills are not only messy to deal with, but they cause pollution and always need an open outdoor setting. Maintaining the optimum temperature and managing the cooking time also needs constant supervision. But that's not the case with this power XL electric grill; now BBQing has become easier than ever. Plug it in, follow the recipe, set the temperature, and cook a luscious meal. Power XL grill has made grilling fun and mess-free experience. It is leading the world of kitchen innovation with its state-of-the-art technology. It has been striving to bring the best of features for an electric grill to the consumers. The great deal about this Electric grill is that they allow you to grill and smoke a variety of food, from red meat to poultry, seafood, vegetables, and even fruits. As the temperature is strictly maintained inside, there are no chances of burning or uneven tenderness.

Benefits of the Power XL Grill

Before getting into the details of the Power XL grill, it is important to understand all the pros of using this smokeless electric grill.

- **Lesser Energy Consumption**

It is wrongly believed that electric grills might add a lot to their electricity bills. Though these grills are completely reliant on an electricity supply, yet they are quite energy efficient in that regard. Its electricity consumption is only 1500 watts, which allows you to cook quickly on variant temperatures from 175 degrees F to 450 degrees F.

- **Non-Stick Grills and Pans**

Gone are the days when you had to spend hours brushing and rubbing the sticky food off a grill before washing it. The power XL electric grill comes with non-stick grilling pans and accessories, which makes after cooking cleaning extremely easy. All you need to do is to lightly scrape the food using a spatula, then wash the pans directly or in the dishwasher.

- **Clean Environment**

There are a lot of electric grills out there that promise smoke-free cooking, but every time you smoke indoors, they fill up your kitchen with a lot of smoke. But thanks to the Power Xl smoke cleaning technology, zero smoke is released into the air, which keeps your kitchen clean all the time.

- **Temperature Control**

The electric heating plates transfers even heat to the grill plate, which cooks evenly charred food every time. The temperature control system keeps the heat inside the grill maintained whether you cover the food with a lid or try open grilling.

- **Great for Beginners**

It is said that grilling delicious and succulent BBQ is not for everybody! Experience matters when it comes to perfect grilling, but the power XL grill has made it easier for all the beginners to grill and smoke a variety of food with complete confidence.

- **User-Friendly and Safe**

Since in an electric grill, you are not required to light any fire on your own, it is much less dangerous than other grills. The wiring is completely insulated, and the entire unit is protected with a solid layering on the outside. With a careful understanding of the device, the Electric grills prove to be user-friendly and safe to use.

- **No Residue**

The charcoal residue, which is usually left behind after an hour's long session of the charcoal grill, makes cleaning really difficult. But when you use the Powder XL grill, there is no such residue, there is only a dripping pan that is easily removable, and you can dispose of the food grease once you are done cooking.

- **Simple Design and Sturdy Built**

One of the best features of the power XL grill is its sturdy exterior and firm built, which makes it safe to use. There is no stand to set it on or legs to make it stand. It's a simple rectangular appliance that can be kept on any countertop surface. When placed carefully over a flat surface, these grills cannot be displaced and stands straight with no imbalance.

Features of the Power XL Grill

Power XL electric grill is a single unit electric device that consists of its electrical heating system, control panel, base unit, and grilling plates. Each component of the device further comprises various features, which are given as follows:

- **Control Panel**

The control panel is relatively simple, and it is present on one side of the grilling chamber. There is a button for POWER and one for FAN; then there is a temperature changing control panel which lets you adjust the heat from 170-450 degrees F. The panel is fitted with LED lights, which makes the keys visible in any dim light setup.

- **Dripping Pan**

The base unit of the grill has the dripping pan or tray, which is placed underneath the racks to capture the drippings of the food being cooked inside. So, whether you are basting the meat with a sauce or oil, the dripping pan catches all the juices and drippings from the food.

- **Grilling Racks**

Each grill is available with an XL size edge to edge surface to fix grilling racks. Each rack is made out of a non-stick surface and is easy to remove, wash, and clean.

CHAPTER 2: GRILLING GUIDE TO USE POWER XL GRILL

Whether you want to grill patties or smoke a juicy rib rack in the Power XL electric grill, now you can do it all using our delicious recipes. But before you get started with the recipes, understand how you can step up this grill and put it to its best use using the following general instructions and guidelines:

How to Step Up the grill

After unboxing your Power XL grill, here is what you need to do next:

• At first, place the power XL grill in a safe place and on a smooth surface. Check if all the components are intact and fixed at their positions.

• The first step after setting the device is to wipe off all the surfaces and wash and dry the cooking pans if you are using it for the first time.

• Plugin the grill carefully, then press the 'Power' button to turn it on.

• Check its temperature settings by pressing the temperature panel and select the required temperature to initiate the preheating.

• The grill starts heating up as soon as the temperature is set. If you want quick preheating, then cover the lid of the grill for 5 minutes, then start cooking.

Preparations:

Before preheating the grill for cooking, it is important to prepare the food and keep it ready to cook. If the meat requires marination, let it completely marinate, then start the heating process. For good results, seasoning and marination are extremely important.

Preheating of the Grill:

It is recommended to preheat the grill at least 15 minutes before cooking the food. First, set the temperature of the grill using the control panel. Place the dripping pan in the bottom of the grill, place the grilling pan on top of the heating element, then cover the lid and allow it to heat up. If you want to add aroma to the food cooking over the grill, then add some water and aromatics like lemon slices or herbs to a tray placed under the grilling pan. And then preheat the grill; in this way, when you are cooking the food on top, it will get all the flavors and aromas of the veggies and aromatic boiled in the water underneath it. Make sure to empty this tray once you are done cooking.

- **Temperature Settings**

Use the optimum cooking temperatures for cooking a particular meal, select high-temperature settings for pork, lamb, and beef, and select low-temperature settings to cook and grill veggies, fruits, seafood, and poultry.

- **Adjust the Food**

Once the desired temperature is achieved, the grill is ready to use. Place the food on the grilling surface and keep track of time while cooking. Select the right position to place the food in the grill. For even cooking, spread the food across the entire surface of the grill and then continue flipping the food pieces after every 5-10 minutes.

- **Basting**

If you are familiar with grilling, then you must also be familiar with the basting process. Every food requires some basting, using sauces or oil, to retain their moisture. Therefore, baste the food after every 10 minutes to keep the meat and other food juicy and succulent, but this step is completely optional and depends on the recipe.

- **Remove the Food**

When the food is cooked, transfer it to a plate. Leave the grilling pan inside the power Xl grill for now.

- **Switch it off**

Once you have removed the food, it's important to switch off the device completely. It is done in two steps. First, you need to press the power button and then unplug the device.

After-Cooking Cleaning

Cleaning prolongs the life of your grill, so it is recommended to clean it thoroughly after every cooking session. Make sure the device is not hot before you initiate cleaning.

- Remove the dripping pan and throw away its residue. Clean the pan by washing it with soap water or wash it in the dishwasher.

- When the grilling pans or other pans are completely cooled, remove them from the base unit and remove all the hard food from the surface by using a soft spatula or scrub. Do not scrub the surface too hard because it is not recommended.

- Rinse and thoroughly wash the grill rack under tap water. Avoid excessive scrubbing. Use normal soap water to wash off the grease, then allow it to dry.

- Or you can place the lid, grilling pans, and racks in the dishwasher, then wash and dry them.

- Wipe off the surface of the grill with a cloth and clean the surface around the grill using a wet cloth.

Precautions:

1. The Power XL grill is an electric grill so avoid placing it over wet surfaces.
2. The base unit must be placed on kitchen counters and sturdy tables, not on grounds.
3. Never plug in the device until all the accessories and plates are set in place.
4. Use the power supply which has a grounded outlet and avoid plugging in during an electrical storm.
5. Do not immerse the base unit in water or avoid any exposure to water or other liquids.
6. Never immerse its power cord in water or liquid.
7. Do not use the device if any of its components are not intact.
8. Keep the power chord away from hot surfaces to avoid any damage.
9. Do not touch the grill while it is hot.

CHAPTER 3: APPETIZER RECIPES

Zucchini Roulades

Preparation Time: 20 minutes

Cooking Time: 12 minutes

Servings: 8

Ingredients:

- 4 medium zucchinis
- 1 cup part-skim ricotta cheese
- ¼ cup Parmesan cheese, grated
- 2 tablespoons fresh basil, minced
- 1 tablespoon Greek olives, chopped
- 1 tablespoon capers, drained
- 1 teaspoon lemon zest, grated
- 1 tablespoon fresh lemon juice
- Salt and ground black pepper, as required

Method:

1. Cut each zucchini into 1/8-inch thick slices lengthwise.
2. Place the water tray in the bottom of Power XL Smokeless Electric Grill.
3. Place about 2 cups of lukewarm water into the water tray.
4. Place the drip pan over water tray and then arrange the heating element.
5. Now, place the grilling pan over heating element.
6. Plugin the Power XL Smokeless Electric Grill and press the 'Power' button to turn it on.
7. Then press 'Fan" button.
8. Set the temperature settings according to manufacturer's directions.
9. After preheating, remove the lid and grease the grilling pan.
10. Place half of the zucchini slices over the grilling pan.
11. Cover with the lid and cook for about 2-3 minutes per side.
12. Transfer the zucchini slices onto a platter.

13. Repeat with the remaining slices.

14. Meanwhile, in a small bowl, place the remaining ingredients and mix well. Set aside.

15. Place about 1 tablespoon of cheese mixture on the end of each zucchini slice.

16. Roll up and secure each with a toothpick.

17. Serve immediately.

Nutritional Information per Serving:

- Calories 70
- Total Fat 3.4 g
- Saturated Fat 1.9 g
- Cholesterol 12 mg
- Sodium 131 mg
- Total Carbs 5.1 g
- Fiber 1.2 g
- Sugar 1.9 g
- Protein 5.8 g

Jalapeño Poppers

Preparation Time: 15 minutes

Cooking Time: 30 minutes

Servings: 12

Ingredients:

- 24 medium jalapeño peppers
- 1 pound uncooked chorizo pork sausage, crumbled
- 2 cups cheddar cheese, shredded
- 12 bacon strips, cut in half

Method:

1. Cut each jalapeno in half lengthwise, about 1/8-inch deep.
2. Then remove the seeds.
3. In a bowl, place the sausage and cheese and mix well.
4. Stuff the jalapeño peppers with cheese mixture and then wrap each with a piece of bacon.
5. With toothpicks, secure each jalapeño pepper.
6. Place the water tray in the bottom of Power XL Smokeless Electric Grill.
7. Place about 2 cups of lukewarm water into the water tray.
8. Place the drip pan over water tray and then, arrange the heating element.
9. Now, place the grilling pan over heating element.
10. Plugin the Power XL Smokeless Electric Grill and press the 'Power' button to turn it on.
11. Then press 'Fan" button.
12. Set the temperature settings according to manufacturer's directions.
13. Cover the grill with lid and let it preheat.
14. After preheating, remove the lid and grease the grilling pan.
15. Place the jalapeño peppers over the grilling pan.
16. Cover with the lid and cook for about 35-40 minutes, flipping once halfway through.
17. Discard the toothpicks and serve warm.

Nutritional Information per Serving:

- Calories 373
- Total Fat 29.5 g
- Saturated Fat 11.4 g
- Cholesterol 83 mg
- Sodium 1800 mg
- Total Carbs 2.7 g
- Fiber 1.1 g
- Sugar 1 g
- Protein 23.2 g

Bacon-Wrapped Asparagus

Preparation Time: 15 minutes

Cooking Time: 12 minutes

Servings: 4

Ingredients:

- 12 fresh asparagus spears, trimmed
- Olive oil cooking spray
- 1/8 teaspoon ground black pepper
- 6 bacon strips, halved lengthwise

Method:

1. Spray the asparagus spears wit cooing spry evenly.
2. Wrap a bacon piece around each asparagus spear and then secure ends with toothpicks.
3. Place the water tray in the bottom of Power XL Smokeless Electric Grill.
4. Place about 2 cups of lukewarm water into the water tray.
5. Place the drip pan over water tray and then arrange the heating element.
6. Now, place the grilling pan over heating element.
7. Plugin the Power XL Smokeless Electric Grill and press the 'Power' button to turn it on.
8. Then press 'Fan" button.
9. Set the temperature settings according to manufacturer's directions.
10. Cover the grill with lid and let it preheat.
11. After preheating, remove the lid and grease the grilling pan.
12. Place the asparagus spears over the grilling pan.
13. Cover with the lid and cook for about 4-6 minutes per side.
14. Discard the toothpicks and serve warm.

Nutritional Information per Serving:

- Calories 250
- Total Fat 18.3 g
- Saturated Fat 6 g
- Cholesterol 48 mg
- Sodium 1004 mg
- Total Carbs 3.5 g
- Fiber 1.5 g
- Sugar 1.4 g
- Protein 17.7 g

Shrimp with Dipping Sauce

Preparation Time: 15 minutes

Cooking Time: 4 minutes

Servings: 6

Ingredients:

- 1½ pounds jumbo shrimp, peeled, deveined, and patted dry
- 2 teaspoons canola oil
- ¼ teaspoon paprika
- Salt and ground black pepper, as required
- ¼ cup warm jalapeño jelly
- ¼ cup chili sauce

Method:

1. Brush the shrimp with oil lightly and then sprinkle with paprika, salt and black pepper.
2. Place the water tray in the bottom of Power XL Smokeless Electric Grill.
3. Place about 2 cups of lukewarm water into the water tray.
4. Place the drip pan over water tray and then, arrange the heating element.
5. Now, place the grilling pan over heating element.
6. Plugin the Power XL Smokeless Electric Grill and press the 'Power' button to turn it on.
7. Then press 'Fan" button.
8. Set the temperature settings according to manufacturer's directions.
9. Cover the grill with lid and let it preheat.
10. After preheating, remove the lid and grease the grilling pan.
11. Place the shrimp over the grilling pan.
12. Cover with the lid and cook for about 2 minutes per side.
13. Meanwhile, in a bowl, place jalapeño jelly and chili sauce and mix well.
14. Serve warm shrimp with dipping sauce.

Nutritional Information per Serving:

- Calories 167
- Total Fat 3.5 g
- Saturated Fat 0.7 g
- Cholesterol 239 mg
- Sodium 584 mg
- Total Carbs 6.6 g
- Fiber 0.1 g
- Sugar 4.1 g
- Protein 25.9 g

Sriracha Wings

Preparation Time: 15 minutes

Cooking Time: 18 minutes

Servings: 8

Ingredients:

For Wings:

- 3 pounds chicken wings
- 1 tablespoon canola oil
- 2 teaspoons ground coriander
- ½ teaspoon garlic salt
- ¼ teaspoon ground black pepper

For Sauce:

- ½ cup fresh orange juice
- 1/3 cup Sriracha chili sauce
- ¼ cup butter, melted
- 3 tablespoons honey
- 2 tablespoons lime juice
- ¼ cup fresh cilantro, chopped

Method:

1. For wings: in a bowl, place all ingredients and toss to coat well.
2. Cover the bowl and refrigerate for about 2 hours or overnight.
3. For sauce: in a bowl, place orange juice, chili sauce, butter, honey and lime juice and mix until well combined. Set aside.
4. Place the water tray in the bottom of Power XL Smokeless Electric Grill.
5. Place about 2 cups of lukewarm water into the water tray.
6. Place the drip pan over water tray and then, arrange the heating element.
7. Now, place the grilling pan over heating element.
8. Plugin the Power XL Smokeless Electric Grill and press the 'Power' button to turn it on.
9. Then press 'Fan" button.
10. Set the temperature settings according to manufacturer's directions.

11. Cover the grill with lid and let it preheat.

12. After preheating, remove the lid and grease the grilling pan.

13. Place the chicken wings over the grilling pan.

14. Cover with the lid and cook for about 15-18 minutes, flipping occasionally.

15. In the last 5 minutes of cooking, brush the wings with some of the sauce.

16. Transfer chicken into the bowl of the remaining sauce and toss to coat.

17. Garnish with cilantro and serve.

Nutritional Information per Serving:

- Calories 432
- Total Fat 20.1 g
- Saturated Fat 7.3 g
- Cholesterol 167 mg
- Sodium 258 mg
- Total Carbs 10.5 g
- Fiber 0.1 g
- Sugar 7.9 g
- Protein 49.5 g

CHAPTER 4: SIDE DISHES RECIPES

Lemony Green Beans

Preparation Time: 10 minutes

Cooking Time: 6 minutes

Servings: 3

Ingredients:

- 2 tablespoons canola oil
- 2 garlic cloves, crushed
- 1 teaspoon red chili powder
- Salt, as required
- 1 pound fresh asparagus, trimmed

Method:

1. In a bowl, place all ingredients except for lemon juice and toss to coat well.
2. Place the water tray in the bottom of Power XL Smokeless Electric Grill.
3. Place about 2 cups of lukewarm water into the water tray.
4. Place the drip pan over water tray and then arrange the heating element.
5. Now, place the grilling pan over heating element.
6. Plugin the Power XL Smokeless Electric Grill and press the 'Power' button to turn it on.
7. Then press 'Fan" button.
8. Set the temperature settings according to manufacturer's directions.
9. Cover the grill with lid and let it preheat.
10. After preheating, remove the lid and grease the grilling pan.
11. Place the asparagus over the grilling pan.
12. Cover with the lid and cook for about 5-6 minutes, turning occasionally.
13. Transfer the green beans into a bowl and drizzle with lemon juice.
14. Serve hot.

Nutritional Information per Serving:

- Calories 118
- Total Fat 9.7 g
- Saturated Fat 0.8 g
- Cholesterol 0mg
- Sodium 63 mg
- Total Carbs 7 g
- Fiber 3.5 g
- Sugar 2.9 g
- Protein 3.6 g

Simple Mushrooms

Preparation Time: 10 minutes

Cooking Time: 5 minutes

Servings: 2

Ingredients:

- 8 ounces shiitake mushrooms, stems discarded
- 1 tablespoon vegetable oil
- 1 garlic clove, minced
- Salt and ground black pepper, as required

Method:

1. In a bowl, place all ingredients and toss to coat well.
2. Place the water tray in the bottom of Power XL Smokeless Electric Grill.
3. Place about 2 cups of lukewarm water into the water tray.
4. Place the drip pan over water tray and then arrange the heating element.
5. Now, place the grilling pan over heating element.
6. Plugin the Power XL Smokeless Electric Grill and press the 'Power' button to turn it on.
7. Then press 'Fan" button.
8. Set the temperature settings according to manufacturer's directions.
9. Cover the grill with lid and let it preheat.
10. After preheating, remove the lid and grease the grilling pan.
11. Place the mushrooms over the grilling pan.
12. Cover with the lid and cook for about 4-5 minutes, turning occasionally.
13. Serve hot.

Nutritional Information per Serving:

- Calories 87
- Total Fat 7.1 g
- Saturated Fat 1.3 g
- Cholesterol 0 mg
- Sodium 84 mg
- Total Carbs 4.2 g
- Fiber 1.2 g
- Sugar 2 g
- Protein 3.7 g

Parmesan Zucchini

Preparation Time: 10 minutes

Cooking Time: 7 minutes

Servings: 4

Ingredients:

- 3 medium zucchinis, cut into ½-inch slices
- 2 tablespoons extra-virgin olive oil
- Salt and ground black pepper, as required
- ¼ cup parmesan cheese, shredded

Method:

1. Brush the zucchini slices with oil and then sprinkle with salt and pepper.
2. Place the water tray in the bottom of Power XL Smokeless Electric Grill.
3. Place about 2 cups of lukewarm water into the water tray.
4. Place the drip pan over water tray and then arrange the heating element.
5. Now, place the grilling pan over heating element.
6. Plugin the Power XL Smokeless Electric Grill and press the 'Power' button to turn it on.
7. Then press 'Fan" button.
8. Set the temperature settings according to manufacturer's directions.
9. Cover the grill with lid and let it preheat.
10. After preheating, remove the lid and grease the grilling pan.
11. Place the zucchini slices over the grilling pan.
12. Cover with the lid and cook for about 5-7 minutes, flipping once halfway through.
13. Transfer the zucchini slices onto a plate and sprinkle with cheese.
14. Serve immediately.

Nutritional Information per Serving:

- Calories 104
- Total Fat 8.6 g
- Saturated Fat 1.9 g
- Cholesterol 4 mg
- Sodium 138 mg
- Total Carbs 5.1 g
- Fiber 1.6 g
- Sugar 2.5 g
- Protein 3.7 g

Balsamic Bell Peppers

Preparation Time: 10 minutes

Cooking Time: 10 minutes

Servings: 4

Ingredients:

- 1 pound small bell peppers, halved and seeded
- 1 tablespoon olive oil
- Salt and ground black pepper, as required
- 1 tablespoon balsamic vinegar

Method:

1. Brush the bell pepper halves with oil and then sprinkle with salt and pepper.
2. Place the water tray in the bottom of Power XL Smokeless Electric Grill.
3. Place about 2 cups of lukewarm water into the water tray.
4. Place the drip pan over water tray and then arrange the heating element.
5. Now, place the grilling pan over heating element.
6. Plugin the Power XL Smokeless Electric Grill and press the 'Power' button to turn it on.
7. Then press 'Fan" button.
8. Set the temperature settings according to manufacturer's directions.
9. Cover the grill with lid and let it preheat.
10. After preheating, remove the lid and grease the grilling pan.
11. Place the bell pepper halves over the grilling pan.
12. Cover with the lid and cook for about 8-10 minutes, flipping once halfway through.
13. Transfer the bell pepper halves onto a plate and drizzle with vinegar.
14. Serve immediately.

Nutritional Information per Serving:

- Calories 40
- Total Fat 3.6 g
- Saturated Fat 0.5 g
- Cholesterol 0mg
- Sodium 40 mg
- Total Carbs 2.3 g
- Fiber 0.4 g
- Sugar 1.5 g
- Protein 0.3 g

Charred Tofu

Preparation Time: 10 minutes

Cooking Time: 15 minutes

Servings: 3

Ingredients:

- 12 ounces extra-firm tofu, pressed, drained and cut into ½-inch thick slices
- Salt and ground black pepper, as required

Method:

1. Season the tofu slices with salt and pepper.
2. Place the water tray in the bottom of Power XL Smokeless Electric Grill.
3. Place about 2 cups of lukewarm water into the water tray.
4. Place the drip pan over water tray and then arrange the heating element.
5. Now, place the grilling pan over heating element.
6. Plugin the Power XL Smokeless Electric Grill and press the 'Power' button to turn it on.
7. Then press 'Fan" button.
8. Set the temperature settings according to manufacturer's directions.
9. Cover the grill with lid and let it preheat.
10. After preheating, remove the lid and grease the grilling pan.
11. Place the mushrooms over the grilling pan.
12. Cover with the lid and cook for about 10-15 minutes, flipping once halfway through.
13. Serve warm.

Nutritional Information per Serving:

- Calories 103
- Total Fat 6.6 g
- Saturated Fat 0.6 g
- Cholesterol 0 mg
- Sodium 59 mg
- Total Carbs 2.3 g
- Fiber 0.5 g
- Sugar 0.6 g
- Protein 11.2 g

CHAPTER 5: POULTRY RECIPES

Seasoned Chicken Breast

Preparation Time: 5 minutes

Cooking Time: 10 minutes

Servings: 4

Ingredients:

- 4 (4-ounce) boneless, skinless chicken breasts
- 1 teaspoon olive oil
- 1 teaspoon jerk seasoning

Method:

1. Brush each chicken breast with olive oil and then rub with jerk seasoning.
2. Place the water tray in the bottom of Power XL Smokeless Electric Grill.
3. Place about 2 cups of lukewarm water into the water tray.
4. Place the drip pan over water tray and then arrange the heating element.
5. Now, place the grilling pan over heating element.
6. Plugin the Power XL Smokeless Electric Grill and press the 'Power' button to turn it on.
7. Then press 'Fan" button.
8. Set the temperature settings according to manufacturer's directions.
9. Cover the grill with lid and let it preheat.
10. After preheating, remove the lid and grease the grilling pan.
11. Place the chicken breasts over the grilling pan.
12. Cover with the lid and cook for about 3-5 minutes per side.
13. Serve hot.

Nutritional Information per Serving:

- Calories 225
- Total Fat 9.6 g
- Saturated Fat 2.5 g
- Cholesterol 101 mg
- Sodium 105 mg
- Total Carbs 0 g
- Fiber 0 g
- Sugar 0 g
- Protein 32.8 g

Marinated Chicken Breasts

Preparation Time: 15 minutes

Cooking Time: 16 minutes

Servings: 4

Ingredients:

- ¼ cup extra-virgin olive oil
- 2 tablespoons fresh lemon juice
- 2 tablespoons maple syrup
- 1 garlic clove, minced
- Salt and ground black pepper, as required
- 4 (6-ounce) boneless, skinless chicken breasts

Method:

1. For marinade: in a large bowl, add oil, lemon juice, maple syrup, garlic, salt and black pepper and beat until well combined.
2. In a large resealable plastic bag, place the chicken and marinade.
3. Seal the bag and shake to coat well.
4. Refrigerate overnight.
5. Place the water tray in the bottom of Power XL Smokeless Electric Grill.
6. Place about 2 cups of lukewarm water into the water tray.
7. Place the drip pan over water tray and then arrange the heating element.
8. Now, place the grilling pan over heating element.
9. Plugin the Power XL Smokeless Electric Grill and press the 'Power' button to turn it on.
10. Then press 'Fan" button.
11. Set the temperature settings according to manufacturer's directions.
12. Cover the grill with lid and let it preheat.
13. After preheating, remove the lid and grease the grilling pan.
14. Place the chicken breasts over the grilling pan.

15. Cover with the lid and cook for about 5-8 minutes per side.

16. Serve hot.

Nutritional Information per Serving:

- Calories 460
- Total Fat 25.3 g
- Saturated Fat 5.3 g
- Cholesterol 151 mg
- Sodium 188 mg
- Total Carbs 7.1 g
- Fiber 0.1 g
- Sugar 6.1 g
- Protein 49.3 g

Spiced Chicken Breasts

Preparation Time: 15 minutes

Cooking Time: 14 minutes

Servings: 4

Ingredients:

- 2 scallions, chopped
- 1 (1-inch) piece fresh ginger, minced
- 2 garlic cloves, minced
- ¼ cup olive oil
- 2 tablespoons fresh lime juice
- 2 tablespoons low-sodium soy sauce
- 1 teaspoon ground cinnamon
- 1 teaspoon ground cumin
- 1 teaspoon ground turmeric
- Ground black pepper, as required
- 4 (5-ounce) boneless, skinless chicken breasts

Method:

1. In a large Ziploc bag, add all the ingredients and seal it.
2. Shake the bag to coat the chicken with marinade well.
3. Refrigerate to marinate for about 20 minutes to 1 hour.
4. Place the water tray in the bottom of Power XL Smokeless Electric Grill.
5. Place about 2 cups of lukewarm water into the water tray.
6. Place the drip pan over water tray and then arrange the heating element.
7. Now, place the grilling pan over heating element.
8. Plugin the Power XL Smokeless Electric Grill and press the 'Power' button to turn it on.
9. Then press 'Fan" button.
10. Set the temperature settings according to manufacturer's directions.
11. Cover the grill with lid and let it preheat.
12. After preheating, remove the lid and grease the grilling pan.
13. Place the chicken breasts over the grilling pan.

14. Cover with the lid and cook for about 6-7 minutes per side

15. Serve hot.

Nutritional Information per Serving:

- Calories 391
- Total Fat 23.3 g
- Saturated Fat 4.7 g
- Cholesterol 126 mg
- Sodium 565 mg
- Total Carbs 2.7 g
- Fiber 0.7 g
- Sugar 0.7 g
- Protein 41.9 g

Peach Glazed Chicken Breasts

Preparation Time: 10 minutes

Cooking Time: 10 minutes

Servings: 4

Ingredients:

For Chicken:

- ¼ teaspoon ground cinnamon
- ¼ teaspoon ground nutmeg
- ¼ teaspoon ground cloves
- Salt, as required
- 4 (5-6-ounce) boneless skinless chicken breasts

For Glaze:

- 1 peach, peeled and pitted
- 1 chipotle in adobo sauce
- 2 tablespoons fresh lemon juice

Method:

1. In a bowl, place spices and salt and mix well.
2. Rub the chicken breasts with the spice mixture evenly.
3. For glaze: in a food processor, place peach, chipotle and lemon juice and pulse until pureed.
4. Transfer into a bowl and set aside.
5. Place the water tray in the bottom of Power XL Smokeless Electric Grill.
6. Place about 2 cups of lukewarm water into the water tray.
7. Place the drip pan over water tray and then arrange the heating element.
8. Now, place the grilling pan over heating element.
9. Plugin the Power XL Smokeless Electric Grill and press the 'Power' button to turn it on.
10. Then press 'Fan" button.
11. Set the temperature settings according to manufacturer's directions.
12. Cover the grill with lid and let it preheat.
13. After preheating, remove the lid and grease the grilling pan.
14. Place the chicken breasts over the grilling pan.

15. Cover with the lid and cook for about 8-10 minutes per side, brushing with the glaze after every 2 minutes.

16. Serve hot.

Nutritional Information per Serving:

- Calories 287
- Total Fat 10.7 g
- Saturated Fat 3 g
- Cholesterol 126 mg
- Sodium 163 mg
- Total Carbs 3.9 g
- Fiber 0.8 g
- Sugar 3.7 g
- Protein 41.5 g

Spicy Chicken Thighs

Preparation Time: 15 minutes

Cooking Time: 18 minutes

Servings: 3

Ingredients:

- 2 tablespoons fresh lime juice
- 1 tablespoon ground chipotle powder
- 1 tablespoon paprika
- 1 tablespoon dried oregano, crushed
- ½ tablespoon garlic powder
- Salt and ground black pepper, as required
- 6 (4-ounce) skinless, boneless chicken thighs

Method:

1. In a bowl, add all ingredients except chicken thighs and mix until well combined.
2. Coat the thighs with spice mixture generously.
3. Place the water tray in the bottom of Power XL Smokeless Electric Grill.
4. Place about 2 cups of lukewarm water into the water tray.
5. Place the drip pan over water tray and then arrange the heating element.
6. Now, place the grilling pan over heating element.
7. Plugin the Power XL Smokeless Electric Grill and press the 'Power' button to turn it on.
8. Then press 'Fan" button.
9. Set the temperature settings according to manufacturer's directions.
10. Cover the grill with lid and let it preheat.
11. After preheating, remove the lid and grease the grilling pan.
12. Place the chicken thighs over the grilling pan.
13. Cover with the lid and cook for about 8 minutes.
14. Carefully change the side and grill for 8-10 minutes more.
15. Serve hot.

Nutritional Information per Serving:

- Calories 300
- Total Fat 8.6 g
- Saturated Fat 3.1 g
- Cholesterol 132 mg
- Sodium 133 mg
- Total Carbs 3.4 g
- Fiber 1.6 g
- Sugar 0.6 g
- Protein 51.4 g

Ketchup Glaze Chicken Thighs

Preparation Time: 15 minutes

Cooking Time: 16 minutes

Servings: 12

Ingredients:

- ½ cup packed brown sugar
- 1/3 cup ketchup
- 1/3 cup low-sodium soy sauce
- 3 tablespoons sherry
- 1½ teaspoons fresh ginger root, minced
- 1½ teaspoons garlic, minced
- 12 (6-ounce) boneless, skinless chicken thighs

Method:

1. In a small bowl, place all ingredients except for chicken thighs and mix well.
2. Transfer about 1 1/3 cups for marinade in another bowl and refrigerate.
3. In a zip lock bag, add the remaining marinade and chicken thighs.
4. Seal the bag and shake to coat well.
5. Refrigerate overnight.
6. Remove the chicken thighs from bag and discard the marinade.
7. Place the water tray in the bottom of Power XL Smokeless Electric Grill.
8. Place about 2 cups of lukewarm water into the water tray.
9. Place the drip pan over water tray and then arrange the heating element.
10. Now, place the grilling pan over heating element.
11. Plugin the Power XL Smokeless Electric Grill and press the 'Power' button to turn it on.
12. Then press 'Fan" button.
13. Set the temperature settings according to manufacturer's directions.
14. Cover the grill with lid and let it preheat.
15. After preheating, remove the lid and grease the grilling pan.
16. Place the chicken thighs over the grilling pan.
17. Cover with the lid and cook for about 6-8 minutes per side.

18. In the last 5 minutes of cooking, baste the chicken thighs with reserved marinade.

19. Serve hot.

Nutritional Information per Serving:

- Calories 359
- Total Fat 12.6 g
- Saturated Fat 3.6 g
- Cholesterol 151 mg
- Sodium 614 mg
- Total Carbs 8.3 g
- Fiber 0 g
- Sugar 7.6 g
- Protein 49.8 g

Chicken Drumsticks

Preparation Time: 10 minutes

Cooking Time: 40 minutes

Servings: 5

Ingredients:

- 2 tablespoons avocado oil
- 1 tablespoon fresh lime juice
- 1 teaspoon red chili powder
- 1 teaspoon garlic powder
- Salt, as required
- 5 (8-ounce) chicken drumsticks

Method:

1. In a mixing bowl, mix avocado oil, lime juice, chili powder and garlic powder and mix well.
2. Add the chicken drumsticks and coat with the marinade generously.
3. Cover the bowl and refrigerate to marinate for about 30-60 minutes.
4. Place the water tray in the bottom of Power XL Smokeless Electric Grill.
5. Place about 2 cups of lukewarm water into the water tray.
6. Place the drip pan over water tray and then arrange the heating element.
7. Now, place the grilling pan over heating element.
8. Plugin the Power XL Smokeless Electric Grill and press the 'Power' button to turn it on.
9. Then press 'Fan" button.
10. Set the temperature settings according to manufacturer's directions.
11. Cover the grill with lid and let it preheat.
12. After preheating, remove the lid and grease the grilling pan.
13. Place the chicken drumsticks over the grilling pan.
14. Cover with the lid and cook for about 30-40 minutes, flipping after every 5 minutes.
15. Serve hot.

Nutritional Information per Serving:

- Calories 395
- Total Fat 13.8 g
- Saturated Fat 3.6 g
- Cholesterol 200 mg
- Sodium 218 mg
- Total Carbs 1 g
- Fiber 0.5 g
- Sugar 0.2 g
- Protein 62.6 g

Glazed Chicken Drumsticks

Preparation Time: 15 minutes

Cooking Time: 25 minutes

Servings: 12

Ingredients:

- 1 (10-ounce) jar red jalapeño pepper jelly
- ¼ cup fresh lime juice
- 12 (6-ounce) chicken drumsticks
- Salt and ground black pepper, as required

Method:

1. In a small saucepan, add jelly and lime juice over medium heat and cook for about 3-5 minutes or until melted.
2. Remove from the heat and set aside.
3. Sprinkle the chicken drumsticks with salt and black pepper.
4. Place the water tray in the bottom of Power XL Smokeless Electric Grill.
5. Place about 2 cups of lukewarm water into the water tray.
6. Place the drip pan over water tray and then arrange the heating element.
7. Now, place the grilling pan over heating element.
8. Plugin the Power XL Smokeless Electric Grill and press the 'Power' button to turn it on.
9. Then press 'Fan" button.
10. Set the temperature settings according to manufacturer's directions.
11. Cover the grill with lid and let it preheat.
12. After preheating, remove the lid and grease the grilling pan.
13. Place the chicken drumsticks over the grilling pan.
14. Cover with the lid and cook for about 15-20 minutes, flipping occasionally.
15. In the last 5 minutes of cooking, baste the chicken thighs with jelly mixture.
16. Serve hot.

Nutritional Information per Serving:

- Calories 359
- Total Fat 9.7 g
- Saturated Fat 2.6 g
- Cholesterol 150 mg
- Sodium 155 mg
- Total Carbs 17.1 g
- Fiber 0 g
- Sugar 11.4 g
- Protein 46.8 g

Marinated Chicken Kabobs

Preparation Time: 15 minutes

Cooking Time: 15 minutes

Servings: 4

Ingredients:

- 1/3 cup extra-virgin olive oil, divided
- 2 garlic cloves, minced
- 1 tablespoon fresh rosemary, minced
- 1 tablespoon fresh oregano, minced
- 1 teaspoon fresh lemon zest, grated
- ½ teaspoon red chili flakes, crushed
- 1 pound boneless, skinless chicken breast, cut into ¾-inch cubes
- 1¾ cups green seedless grapes, rinsed
- ½ teaspoon salt
- 1 tablespoon fresh lemon juice

Method:

1. In small bowl, add ¼ cup of oil, garlic, fresh herbs, lemon zest and chili flakes and beat until well combined.
2. Thread the chicken cubes and grapes onto 12 metal skewers.
3. In a large baking dish, arrange the skewers.
4. Place the marinade and mix well.
5. Refrigerate to marinate for about 4-24 hours.
6. Place the water tray in the bottom of Power XL Smokeless Electric Grill.
7. Place about 2 cups of lukewarm water into the water tray.
8. Place the drip pan over water tray and then arrange the heating element.
9. Now, place the grilling pan over heating element.
10. Plugin the Power XL Smokeless Electric Grill and press the 'Power' button to turn it on.
11. Then press 'Fan" button.
12. Set the temperature settings according to manufacturer's directions.
13. Cover the grill with lid and let it preheat.

14. After preheating, remove the lid and grease the grilling pan.

15. Place the chicken skewers over the grilling pan.

16. Cover with the lid and cook for about 3-5 minutes per side or until chicken is done completely.

17. Remove from the grill and transfer the skewers onto a serving platter.

18. Drizzle with lemon juice and remaining oil and serve.

Nutritional Information per Serving:

- Calories 310
- Total Fat 20.1 g
- Saturated Fat 2.6 g
- Cholesterol 73 mg
- Sodium 351 mg
- Total Carbs 8.8 g
- Fiber 1.3 g
- Sugar 6.7 g
- Protein 24.6 g

Meatballs Kabobs

Preparation Time: 15 minutes

Cooking Time: 14 minutes

Servings: 4

Ingredients:

- 1 yellow onion, chopped roughly
- ½ cup lemongrass, chopped roughly
- 2 garlic cloves, chopped roughly
- 1½ pounds lean ground turkey
- 1 teaspoon sesame oil
- ½ tablespoons low-sodium soy sauce
- 1 tablespoon arrowroot starch
- 1/8 teaspoons powdered stevia
- Salt and ground black pepper, as required

Method:

1. In a food processor, add the onion, lemongrass and garlic and pulse until chopped finely.
2. Transfer the onion mixture into a large bowl.
3. Add the remaining ingredients and mix until well combined.
4. Make 12 equal sized balls from meat mixture.
5. Thread the balls onto the presoaked wooden skewers.
6. Place the water tray in the bottom of Power XL Smokeless Electric Grill.
7. Place about 2 cups of lukewarm water into the water tray.
8. Place the drip pan over water tray and then arrange the heating element.
9. Now, place the grilling pan over heating element.
10. Plugin the Power XL Smokeless Electric Grill and press the 'Power' button to turn it on.
11. Then press 'Fan" button.
12. Set the temperature settings according to manufacturer's directions.
13. Cover the grill with lid and let it preheat.
14. After preheating, remove the lid and grease the grilling pan.
15. Place the skewers over the grilling pan.

16. Cover with the lid and cook for about 6-7 minutes per side.

17. Serve hot.

Nutritional Information per Serving:

- Calories 276
- Total Fat 13.4 g
- Saturated Fat 4 g
- Cholesterol 122 mg
- Sodium 280 mg
- Total Carbs 5.6 g
- Fiber 0.6 g
- Sugar 1.3 g
- Protein 34.2 g

Thyme Duck Breasts

Preparation Time: 10 minutes

Cooking Time: 16 minutes

Servings: 2

Ingredients:

- 2 shallots, sliced thinly
- 1 tablespoon fresh ginger, minced
- 2 tablespoons fresh thyme, chopped
- Salt and ground black pepper, as required
- 2 duck breasts

Method:

1. In a large bowl, place the shallots, ginger, thyme, salt, and black pepper, and mix well.
2. Add the duck breasts and coat with marinade evenly.
3. Refrigerate to marinate for about 2-12 hours.
4. Place the water tray in the bottom of Power XL Smokeless Electric Grill.
5. Place about 2 cups of lukewarm water into the water tray.
6. Place the drip pan over water tray and then arrange the heating element.
7. Now, place the grilling pan over heating element.
8. Plugin the Power XL Smokeless Electric Grill and press the 'Power' button to turn it on.
9. Then press 'Fan" button.
10. Set the temperature settings according to manufacturer's directions.
11. Cover the grill with lid and let it preheat.
12. After preheating, remove the lid and grease the grilling pan, skin-side down.
13. Place the duck breast over the grilling pan.
14. Cover with the lid and cook for about 6-8 minutes per side.
15. Serve hot.

Nutritional Information per Serving:

- Calories 337
- Total Fat 10.1 g
- Saturated Fat 0 g
- Cholesterol 0 mg
- Sodium 80 mg
- Total Carbs 3.4 g
- Fiber 0 g
- Sugar 0.1 g
- Protein 55.5 g

CHAPTER 6: RED MEAT RECIPES

Filet Mignon

Preparation Time: 5 minutes

Cooking Time: 10 minutes

Servings: 2

Ingredients:

- 2 filet mignons
- Salt and ground black pepper, as required

Method:

1. Season the filet mignons with salt and black pepper generously.
2. Place the water tray in the bottom of Power XL Smokeless Electric Grill.
3. Place about 2 cups of lukewarm water into the water tray.
4. Place the drip pan over water tray and then arrange the heating element.
5. Now, place the grilling pan over heating element.
6. Plugin the Power XL Smokeless Electric Grill and press the 'Power' button to turn it on.
7. Then press 'Fan" button.
8. Set the temperature settings according to manufacturer's directions.
9. Cover the grill with lid and let it preheat.
10. After preheating, remove the lid and grease the grilling pan.
11. Place the filet mignons over the grilling pan.
12. Cover with the lid and cook for about 5 minutes per side.
13. Serve immediately.

Nutritional Information per Serving:

- Calories 304
- Total Fat 11.2 g
- Saturated Fat 4.3 g
- Cholesterol 112 mg
- Sodium 178 mg
- Total Carbs 0 g
- Fiber 0 g
- Sugar 0 g
- Protein 47.8 g

Garlicky Flank Steak

Preparation Time: 15 minutes

Cooking Time: 15 minutes

Servings: 6

Ingredients:

- 3 garlic cloves, minced
- 2 tablespoons fresh rosemary, chopped
- Salt and ground black pepper, as required
- 2 pounds flank steak, trimmed

Method:

1. In a large bowl, add all the ingredients except the steak and mix until well combined.
2. Add the steak and coat with the mixture generously.
3. Set aside for about 10 minutes.
4. Place the water tray in the bottom of Power XL Smokeless Electric Grill.
5. Place about 2 cups of lukewarm water into the water tray.
6. Place the drip pan over water tray and then arrange the heating element.
7. Now, place the grilling pan over heating element.
8. Plugin the Power XL Smokeless Electric Grill and press the 'Power' button to turn it on.
9. Then press 'Fan" button.
10. Set the temperature settings according to manufacturer's directions.
11. Cover the grill with lid and let it preheat.
12. After preheating, remove the lid and grease the grilling pan.
13. Place the steak over the grilling pan.
14. Cover with the lid and cook for about 12-15 minutes, flipping after every 3-4 minutes.
15. Remove from the grill and place the steak onto a cutting board for about 5 minutes.
16. With a sharp knife, cut the steak into desired sized slices and serve.

Nutritional Information per Serving:

- Calories 299
- Total Fat 12.8 g
- Saturated Fat 5.3 g
- Cholesterol 83 mg
- Sodium 113 mg
- Total Carbs 1.2 g
- Fiber 0.5 g
- Sugar 0 g
- Protein 42.2 g

Beef Skewers

Preparation Time: 15 minutes

Cooking Time: 8 minutes

Servings: 6

Ingredients:

- 3 garlic cloves, minced
- 1 tablespoon fresh lemon zest, grated
- 2 teaspoons fresh rosemary, minced
- 2 teaspoons fresh parsley, minced
- 2 teaspoons fresh oregano, minced
- 2 teaspoons fresh thyme, minced
- 4 tablespoons olive oil
- 2 tablespoons fresh lemon juice
- Salt and ground black pepper, as required
- 2 pounds beef sirloin, cut into cubes

Method:

1. In a bowl, add all the ingredients except the beef and mix well.
2. Add the beef and coat with the herb mixture generously.
3. Refrigerate to marinate for at least 20-30 minutes.
4. Remove the beef cubes from the marinade and thread onto metal skewers.
5. Place the water tray in the bottom of Power XL Smokeless Electric Grill.
6. Place about 2 cups of lukewarm water into the water tray.
7. Place the drip pan over water tray and then arrange the heating element.
8. Now, place the grilling pan over heating element.
9. Plugin the Power XL Smokeless Electric Grill and press the 'Power' button to turn it on.
10. Then press 'Fan" button.
11. Set the temperature settings according to manufacturer's directions.
12. Cover the grill with lid and let it preheat.
13. After preheating, remove the lid and grease the grilling pan.
14. Place the skewers over the grilling pan.

15. Cover with the lid and cook for about 6-8 minutes, flipping after every 2 minutes.

16. Remove from the grill and place onto a platter for about 5 minutes before serving.

Nutritional Information per Serving:

- Calories 369
- Total Fat 18.9 g
- Saturated Fat 5 g
- Cholesterol 135 mg
- Sodium 129 mg
- Total Carbs 1.6 g
- Fiber 0.6 g
- Sugar 0.2 g
- Protein 46.2 g

Spicy Pork Chops

Preparation Time: 10 minutes

Cooking Time: 15 minutes

Servings: 4

Ingredients:

- 2 teaspoons Worcestershire sauce
- 1 teaspoon liquid smoke flavoring
- 1 tablespoon onion powder
- 1 tablespoon garlic powder
- 1 tablespoon paprika
- 1 tablespoon seasoned salt
- 1 teaspoon freshly ground black pepper
- 4 (½-¾-inch thick) bone-in pork chops

Method:

1. In a bowl, mix together all ingredients except for chops.
2. Add chops and coat with mixture generously.
3. Set aside for about 10-15 minutes.
4. Place the water tray in the bottom of Power XL Smokeless Electric Grill.
5. Place about 2 cups of lukewarm water into the water tray.
6. Place the drip pan over water tray and then arrange the heating element.
7. Now, place the grilling pan over heating element.
8. Plugin the Power XL Smokeless Electric Grill and press the 'Power' button to turn it on.
9. Then press 'Fan" button.
10. Set the temperature settings according to manufacturer's directions.
11. Cover the grill with lid and let it preheat.
12. After preheating, remove the lid and grease the grilling pan.
13. Place the chops over the grilling pan.
14. Cover with the lid and cook for about 15 minutes, flipping once halfway through.
15. Serve hot.

Nutritional Information per Serving:

- Calories 262
- Total Fat 12.3 g
- Saturated Fat 4.1 g
- Cholesterol 85 mg
- Sodium 1800 mg
- Total Carbs 5.7 g
- Fiber 1.1 g
- Sugar 2.8 g
- Protein 29.9 g

Glazed Pork Chops

Preparation Time: 10 minutes

Cooking Time: 12 minutes

Servings: 6

Ingredients:

- 2 tablespoons fresh ginger root, minced
- 1 teaspoon garlic, minced
- 2 tablespoons fresh orange zest, grated finely
- ½ cup fresh orange juice
- 1 teaspoon garlic chile paste
- 2 tablespoons soy sauce
- Salt, as required
- 6 (½-inch thick) pork loin chops

Method:

1. In a large bowl, mix together all ingredients except for chops.
2. Add chops and coat with marinade generously.
3. Cover and refrigerate to marinate for about 2 hours, tossing occasionally.
4. Place the water tray in the bottom of Power XL Smokeless Electric Grill.
5. Place about 2 cups of lukewarm water into the water tray.
6. Place the drip pan over water tray and then arrange the heating element.
7. Now, place the grilling pan over heating element.
8. Plugin the Power XL Smokeless Electric Grill and press the 'Power' button to turn it on.
9. Then press 'Fan" button.
10. Set the temperature settings according to manufacturer's directions.
11. Cover the grill with lid and let it preheat.
12. After preheating, remove the lid and grease the grilling pan.
13. Place the chops over the grilling pan.
14. Cover with the lid and cook for about 10-12 minutes, flipping once in the middle way or until desired doneness.
15. Serve hot.

Nutritional Information per Serving:

- Calories 560
- Total Fat 42.3 g
- Saturated Fat 15.9 g
- Cholesterol 146 mg
- Sodium 447 mg
- Total Carbs 3.5 g
- Fiber 0.3 g
- Sugar 1.9 g
- Protein 38.8 g

Prosciutto-Wrapped Pork Chops

Preparation Time: 15 minutes

Cooking Time: 14 minutes

Servings: 4

Ingredients:

- 4 (6-ounce) boneless pork chops
- Salt and ground black pepper, as required
- 8 fresh sage leaves
- 8 thin prosciutto slices
- 2 tablespoons olive oil

Method:

1. Season the pork chops with salt and black pepper evenly.
2. Arrange 2 sage leaves over each pork chop.
3. Wrap each pork chop with 2 prosciutto slices.
4. Lightly brush both sides of chops with olive oil.
5. Place the water tray in the bottom of Power XL Smokeless Electric Grill.
6. Place about 2 cups of lukewarm water into the water tray.
7. Place the drip pan over water tray and then arrange the heating element.
8. Now, place the grilling pan over heating element.
9. Plugin the Power XL Smokeless Electric Grill and press the 'Power' button to turn it on.
10. Then press 'Fan" button.
11. Set the temperature settings according to manufacturer's directions.
12. Cover the grill with lid and let it preheat.
13. After preheating, remove the lid and grease the grilling pan.
14. Place the chops over the grilling pan.
15. Cover with the lid and cook for about 6-7 minutes per side.
16. Serves hot.

Nutritional Information per Serving:

- Calories 384
- Total Fat 16.1 g
- Saturated Fat 4.1 g
- Cholesterol 154 mg
- Sodium 809 mg
- Total Carbs 0.8 g
- Fiber 0 g
- Sugar 0 g
- Protein 56.2 g

Spiced Pork Tenderloin

Preparation Time: 15 minutes

Cooking Time: 18 minutes

Servings: 6

Ingredients:

- 2 teaspoons fennel seeds
- 2 teaspoons coriander seeds
- 2 teaspoons caraway seeds
- 1 teaspoon cumin seeds
- 1 bay leaf
- Salt and freshly ground black pepper, to taste
- 2 tablespoons fresh dill, chopped
- 2 (1-pound) pork tenderloins, trimmed

Method:

1. For spice rub: in a spice grinder, add the seeds and bay leaf and grind until finely powdered.
2. Add the salt and black pepper and mix.
3. In a small bowl, reserve 2 tablespoons of spice rub.
4. In another small bowl, mix together the remaining spice rub, and dill.
5. Place 1 tenderloin onto a piece of plastic wrap.
6. With a sharp knife, slice through the meat to within ½-inch of the opposite side. Now, open the tenderloin like a book.
7. Cover with another plastic wrap and with a meat pounder, gently pound into ½-inch thickness.
8. Repeat with the remaining tenderloin.
9. Remove the plastic wrap and spread half of the spice and dill mixture over the center of each tenderloin.
10. Roll each tenderloin like a cylinder.
11. With a kitchen string, tightly tie each roll at several places.
12. Rub each roll with the reserved spice rub generously.
13. With 1 plastic wrap, wrap each roll and refrigerate for at least 4-6 hours.
14. Place the water tray in the bottom of Power XL Smokeless Electric Grill.
15. Place about 2 cups of lukewarm water into the water tray.

16. Place the drip pan over water tray and then arrange the heating element.
17. Now, place the grilling pan over heating element.
18. Plugin the Power XL Smokeless Electric Grill and press the 'Power' button to turn it on.
19. Then press 'Fan" button.
20. Set the temperature settings according to manufacturer's directions.
21. Cover the grill with lid and let it preheat.
22. After preheating, remove the lid and grease the grilling pan.
23. Remove the plastic wrap from tenderloins.
24. Place the tenderloins over the grilling pan.
25. Cover with the lid and cook for about 14-18 minutes, flipping occasionally.
26. Remove from the grill and place tenderloins onto a cutting board.
27. With a piece of foil, cover each tenderloin for at least 5-10 minutes before slicing.
28. With a sharp knife, cut the tenderloins into desired size slices and serve.

Nutritional Information per Serving:

- Calories 313
- Total Fat 12.6 g
- Saturated Fat 4.4 g
- Cholesterol 142 mg
- Sodium 127 mg
- Total Carbs 1.4 g
- Fiber 0.7 g
- Sugar 0 g
- Protein 45.7 g

Pork Kabobs

Preparation Time: 15 minutes

Cooking Time: 10 minutes

Servings: 6

Ingredients:

- 1 tablespoon smoked paprika
- 1 teaspoon onion powder
- ½ teaspoon garlic powder
- ¼ teaspoon cayenne pepper
- Salt and ground black pepper, as required
- 2 (¾-pound) pork tenderloins, trimmed and cut into 1-inch cubes
- ¼ cup balsamic vinegar
- 3 tablespoons honey
- 1 tablespoon Dijon mustard
- 2 teaspoons olive oil
- 12 dried figs, halved

Method:

1. In a bowl, mix together the spices, salt and black pepper.
2. Add pork cubes and coat with the spice mixture generously.
3. Cover the bowl and refrigerate for about 30 minutes.
4. For glaze: in a bowl, place vinegar, honey, mustard and oil and beat until well combined.
5. Thread the pork cubes and fig halves onto pre-soaked wooden skewers.
6. Place the water tray in the bottom of Power XL Smokeless Electric Grill.
7. Place about 2 cups of lukewarm water into the water tray.
8. Place the drip pan over water tray and then arrange the heating element.
9. Now, place the grilling pan over heating element.
10. Plugin the Power XL Smokeless Electric Grill and press the 'Power' button to turn it on.
11. Then press 'Fan" button.
12. Set the temperature settings according to manufacturer's directions.
13. Cover the grill with lid and let it preheat.

14. After preheating, remove the lid and grease the grilling pan.

15. Place the skewers over the grilling pan.

16. Cover with the lid and cook for about 8-10 minutes, flipping and basting with glaze occasionally.

17. Serve hot.

Nutritional Information per Serving:

- Calories 377
- Total Fat 11.4 g
- Saturated Fat 3.6 g
- Cholesterol 107 mg
- Sodium 135 mg
- Total Carbs 34.3 g
- Fiber 4.3 g
- Sugar 27.2 g
- Protein 35.5 g

Lamb Steak

Preparation Time: 10 minutes

Cooking Time: 4 minutes

Servings: 6

Ingredients:

- 2 garlic cloves, minced
- 2 tablespoons olive oil
- 2 teaspoons dried oregano, crushed
- 2 tablespoons sumac
- 2 teaspoons sweet paprika
- 12 lamb cutlets, trimmed

Method:

1. In a bowl mix together all ingredients except for lamb cutlets.
2. Add the cutlets and coat with garlic mixture evenly.
3. Set aside for at least 10 minutes.
4. Place the water tray in the bottom of Power XL Smokeless Electric Grill.
5. Place about 2 cups of lukewarm water into the water tray.
6. Place the drip pan over water tray and then arrange the heating element.
7. Now, place the grilling pan over heating element.
8. Plugin the Power XL Smokeless Electric Grill and press the 'Power' button to turn it on.
9. Then press 'Fan" button.
10. Set the temperature settings according to manufacturer's directions.
11. Cover the grill with lid and let it preheat.
12. After preheating, remove the lid and grease the grilling pan.
13. Place the cutlets over the grilling pan.
14. Cover with the lid and cook for about 2 minutes from both sides or until desired doneness.
15. Serve hot.

Nutritional Information per Serving:

- Calories 343
- Total Fat 16.6 g
- Saturated Fat 4.9 g
- Cholesterol 144 mg
- Sodium 122 mg
- Total Carbs 1 g
- Fiber 0.5 g
- Sugar 0.1 g
- Protein 45.2 g

Garlicy Lamb Chops

Preparation Time: 10 minutes

Cooking Time: 6 minutes

Servings: 4

Ingredients:

- 1 tablespoon fresh ginger, grated
- 4 garlic cloves, chopped roughly
- 1 teaspoon ground cumin
- ½ teaspoon red chili powder
- Salt and ground black pepper, as required
- 1 tablespoon olive oil
- 1 tablespoon fresh lemon juice
- 8 lamb chops, trimmed

Method:

1. In a bowl, mix together all ingredients except for chops.
2. With a hand blender, blend until a smooth mixture forms.
3. Add the chops and coat with mixture generously.
4. Refrigerate to marinate for overnight.
5. Place the water tray in the bottom of Power XL Smokeless Electric Grill.
6. Place about 2 cups of lukewarm water into the water tray.
7. Place the drip pan over water tray and then arrange the heating element.
8. Now, place the grilling pan over heating element.
9. Plugin the Power XL Smokeless Electric Grill and press the 'Power' button to turn it on.
10. Then press 'Fan" button.
11. Set the temperature settings according to manufacturer's directions.
12. Cover the grill with lid and let it preheat.
13. After preheating, remove the lid and grease the grilling pan.
14. Place the lamb chops over the grilling pan.
15. Cover with the lid and cook for about 3 minutes per side.
16. Serve hot.

Nutritional Information per Serving:

- Calories 465
- Total Fat 20.4 g
- Saturated Fat 6.5 g
- Cholesterol 204 mg
- Sodium 178 mg
- Total Carbs 2.4 g
- Fiber 0.4 g
- Sugar 0.2 g
- Protein 64.2 g

Rosemary Lamb Chops

Preparation Time: 10 minutes

Cooking Time: 10 minutes

Servings: 2

Ingredients:

- 1 tablespoon olive oil
- 1 tablespoon fresh lemon juice
- 1 tablespoon fresh rosemary, chopped
- ½ teaspoon garlic, minced
- Salt and ground black pepper, as required
- 2 (8-ounce) (½-inch-thick) lamb shoulder blade chops

Method:

1. In a bowl, place all ingredients and beat until well combined.
2. Place the chops and oat with the mixture well.
3. Seal the bag and shake vigorously to coat evenly.
4. Place the water tray in the bottom of Power XL Smokeless Electric Grill.
5. Place about 2 cups of lukewarm water into the water tray.
6. Place the drip pan over water tray and then arrange the heating element.
7. Now, place the grilling pan over heating element.
8. Plugin the Power XL Smokeless Electric Grill and press the 'Power' button to turn it on.
9. Then press 'Fan" button.
10. Set the temperature settings according to manufacturer's directions.
11. Cover the grill with lid and let it preheat.
12. After preheating, remove the lid and grease the grilling pan.
13. Place the lamb chops over the grilling pan.
14. Cover with the lid and cook for about 4-5 minutes per side.
15. Serve hot.

Nutritional Information per Serving:

- Calories 410
- Total Fat 25.4 g
- Saturated Fat 7.2 g
- Cholesterol 151 mg
- Sodium 241 mg
- Total Carbs 1.5 g
- Fiber 0.7 g
- Sugar 0.2 g
- Protein 44.3 g

Spiced Lamb Chops

Preparation Time: 10 minutes

Cooking Time: 8 minutes

Servings: 8

Ingredients:

- 1 tablespoon fresh mint leaves, chopped
- 1 teaspoon garlic paste
- 1 teaspoon ground allspice
- ½ teaspoon ground nutmeg
- ½ teaspoon ground green cardamom
- ¼ teaspoon hot paprika
- Salt and ground black pepper, as required
- 4 tablespoons olive oil
- 2 tablespoons fresh lemon juice
- 2 racks of lamb, trimmed and separated into 16 chops

Method:

1. In a large bowl, add all the ingredients except for chops and mix until well combined.
2. Add the chops and coat with the mixture generously.
3. Refrigerate to marinate for about 5-6 hours.
4. Place the water tray in the bottom of Power XL Smokeless Electric Grill.
5. Place about 2 cups of lukewarm water into the water tray.
6. Place the drip pan over water tray and then arrange the heating element.
7. Now, place the grilling pan over heating element.
8. Plugin the Power XL Smokeless Electric Grill and press the 'Power' button to turn it on.
9. Then press 'Fan" button.
10. Set the temperature settings according to manufacturer's directions.
11. Cover the grill with lid and let it preheat.
12. After preheating, remove the lid and grease the grilling pan.
13. Place the lamb chops over the grilling pan.
14. Cover with the lid and cook for about 6-8 minutes, flipping once halfway through.

15. Serve hot.

Nutritional Information per Serving:

- Calories 380
- Total Fat 19.6 g
- Saturated Fat 5.6 g
- Cholesterol 153 mg
- Sodium 150 mg
- Total Carbs 0.5 g
- Fiber 0.2 g
- Sugar 0.1 g
- Protein 47.9 g

Lamb Kabobs

Preparation Time: 15 minutes

Cooking Time: 10 minutes

Servings: 6

Ingredients:

- 1 large pineapple, cubed into 1½-inch size, divided
- 1 (½-inch) piece fresh ginger, chopped
- 2 garlic cloves, chopped
- Salt, as required
- 16-24-ounce lamb shoulder steak, trimmed and cubed into 1½-inch size
- Fresh mint leaves from a bunch
- Ground cinnamon, as required

Method:

1. In a food processor, add about 1½ cups of pineapple, ginger, garlic and salt and pulse until smooth.
2. Transfer the mixture into a large bowl.
3. Add the chops and coat with mixture generously.
4. Refrigerate to marinate for about 1-2 hours.
5. Remove from the refrigerator.
6. Thread lamb cubes, remaining pineapple and mint leaves onto pre-soaked wooden skewers.
7. Place the water tray in the bottom of Power XL Smokeless Electric Grill.
8. Place about 2 cups of lukewarm water into the water tray.
9. Place the drip pan over water tray and then arrange the heating element.
10. Now, place the grilling pan over heating element.
11. Plugin the Power XL Smokeless Electric Grill and press the 'Power' button to turn it on.
12. Then press 'Fan" button.
13. Set the temperature settings according to manufacturer's directions.
14. Cover the grill with lid and let it preheat.
15. After preheating, remove the lid and grease the grilling pan.
16. Place the skewers over the grilling pan.
17. Cover with the lid and cook for about 10 minutes, turning occasionally.

Nutritional Information per Serving:

- Calories 288
- Total Fat 8.5 g
- Saturated Fat 3 g
- Cholesterol 102 mg
- Sodium 115 mg
- Total Carbs 20.2 g
- Fiber 2.1 g
- Sugar 14.9 g
- Protein 32.7 g

CHAPTER 7: FISH RECIPES

Herbed Salmon

Preparation Time: 10 minutes

Cooking Time: 8 minutes

Servings: 4

Ingredients:

- 2 garlic cloves, minced
- 1 teaspoon dried oregano, crushed
- 1 teaspoon dried basil, crushed
- Salt and ground black pepper, as required
- ¼ cup olive oil
- 2 tablespoons fresh lemon juice
- 4 (4-ounce) salmon fillets

Method:

1. In a large bowl, add all ingredients except for salmon and mix well.
2. Add the salmon and coat with marinade generously.
3. Cover and refrigerate to marinate for at least 1 hour.
4. Place the water tray in the bottom of Power XL Smokeless Electric Grill.
5. Place about 2 cups of lukewarm water into the water tray.
6. Place the drip pan over water tray and then arrange the heating element.
7. Now, place the grilling pan over heating element.
8. Plugin the Power XL Smokeless Electric Grill and press the 'Power' button to turn it on.
9. Then press 'Fan" button.
10. Set the temperature settings according to manufacturer's directions.
11. Cover the grill with lid and let it preheat.
12. After preheating, remove the lid and grease the grilling pan.
13. Place the salmon fillets over the grilling pan.
14. Cover with the lid and cook for about 4 minutes per side.

15. Serve hot.

Nutritional Information per Serving:

- Calories 263
- Total Fat 19.7 g
- Saturated Fat 2.9 g
- Cholesterol 50 mg
- Sodium 91 mg
- Total Carbs 0.9 g
- Fiber 0.2 g
- Sugar 0.2 g
- Protein 22.2 g

Lemony Salmon

Preparation Time: 10 minutes

Cooking Time: 14 minutes

Servings: 4

Ingredients:

- 2 garlic cloves, minced
- 1 tablespoon fresh lemon zest, grated
- 2 tablespoons butter, melted
- 2 tablespoons fresh lemon juice
- Salt and ground black pepper, as required
- 4 (6-ounce) boneless, skinless salmon fillets

Method:

1. In a bowl, place all ingredients (except salmon fillets) and mix well.
2. Add the salmon fillets and coat with garlic mixture generously.
3. Place the water tray in the bottom of Power XL Smokeless Electric Grill.
4. Place about 2 cups of lukewarm water into the water tray.
5. Place the drip pan over water tray and then arrange the heating element.
6. Now, place the grilling pan over heating element.
7. Plugin the Power XL Smokeless Electric Grill and press the 'Power' button to turn it on.
8. Then press 'Fan" button.
9. Set the temperature settings according to manufacturer's directions.
10. Cover the grill with lid and let it preheat.
11. After preheating, remove the lid and grease the grilling pan.
12. Place the salmon fillets over the grilling pan.
13. Cover with the lid and cook for about 6-7 minutes per side.
14. Serve immediately.

Nutritional Information per Serving:

- Calories 281
- Total Fat 16.3 g
- Saturated Fat 5.2 g
- Cholesterol 90 mg
- Sodium 157 mg
- Total Carbs 1 g
- Fiber 0.2 g
- Sugar 0.3 g
- Protein 33.3 g

Soy Sauce Salmon

Preparation Time: 10 minutes

Cooking Time: 10 minutes

Servings: 4

Ingredients:

- 2 tablespoons scallions, chopped
- ¾ teaspoon fresh ginger, minced
- 1 garlic clove, minced
- ½ teaspoon dried dill weed, crushed
- ¼ cup olive oil
- 2 tablespoons balsamic vinegar
- 2 tablespoons low-sodium soy sauce
- 4 (5-ounce) boneless salmon fillets

Method:

1. Add all ingredients except for salmon in a large bowl and mix well.
2. Add salmon and coat with marinade generously.
3. Cover and refrigerate to marinate for at least 4-5 hours.
4. Place the water tray in the bottom of Power XL Smokeless Electric Grill.
5. Place about 2 cups of lukewarm water into the water tray.
6. Place the drip pan over water tray and then arrange the heating element.
7. Now, place the grilling pan over heating element.
8. Plugin the Power XL Smokeless Electric Grill and press the 'Power' button to turn it on.
9. Then press 'Fan" button.
10. Set the temperature settings according to manufacturer's directions.
11. Cover the grill with lid and let it preheat.

12. After preheating, remove the lid and grease the grilling pan.

13. Place the salmon fillets over the grilling pan.

14. Cover with the lid and cook for about 5 minutes per side.

15. Serve hot.

Nutritional Information per Serving:

- Calories 303

- Total Fat 21.4 g

- Saturated Fat 3.1 g

- Cholesterol 63 mg

- Sodium 504 mg

- Total Carbs 1.4 g

- Fiber 0.2 g

- Sugar 0.6 g

- Protein 28.2 g

Lemony Cod

Preparation Time: 10 minutes

Cooking Time: 14 minutes

Servings: 2

Ingredients:

- 1 garlic cloves, minced
- ½ tablespoon fresh olive oil
- 1 tablespoon fresh lemon juice
- ½ teaspoon dried rosemary, crushed
- ¼ teaspoon paprika
- Salt and ground black pepper, as required
- 2 (6-ounce) skinless, boneless cod fillets

Method:

1. In a large bowl, mix together all ingredients except cod fillets.
2. Add the cod fillets and coat with garlic mixture generously.
3. Place the water tray in the bottom of Power XL Smokeless Electric Grill.
4. Place about 2 cups of lukewarm water into the water tray.
5. Place the drip pan over water tray and then arrange the heating element.
6. Now, place the grilling pan over heating element.
7. Plugin the Power XL Smokeless Electric Grill and press the 'Power' button to turn it on.
8. Then press 'Fan" button.
9. Set the temperature settings according to manufacturer's directions.
10. Cover the grill with lid and let it preheat.
11. After preheating, remove the lid and grease the grilling pan.
12. Place the cod fillets over the grilling pan.
13. Cover with the lid and cook for about 6-7 minutes per side.
14. Serve hot.

Nutritional Information per Serving:

- Calories 173
- Total Fat 5.2 g
- Saturated Fat 0.6 g
- Cholesterol 84 mg
- Sodium 186 mg
- Total Carbs 1 g
- Fiber 0.3 g
- Sugar 0.2 g
- Protein 30.6 g

Simple Mahi-Mahi

Preparation Time: 10 minutes

Cooking Time: 10 minutes

Servings: 4

Ingredients:

- 4 (6-ounce) mahi-mahi fillets
- 2 tablespoons olive oil
- Salt and ground black pepper, as required

Method:

1. Coat fish fillets with olive oil and season with salt and black pepper evenly.
2. Place the water tray in the bottom of Power XL Smokeless Electric Grill.
3. Place about 2 cups of lukewarm water into the water tray.
4. Place the drip pan over water tray and then arrange the heating element.
5. Now, place the grilling pan over heating element.
6. Plugin the Power XL Smokeless Electric Grill and press the 'Power' button to turn it on.
7. Then press 'Fan" button.
8. Set the temperature settings according to manufacturer's directions.
9. Cover the grill with lid and let it preheat.
10. After preheating, remove the lid and grease the grilling pan.
11. Place the fish fillets over the grilling pan.
12. Cover with the lid and cook for about 5 minutes per side.
13. Serve hot.

Nutritional Information per Serving:

- Calories 195
- Total Fat 7 g
- Saturated Fat 1 g
- Cholesterol 60 mg
- Sodium 182 mg
- Total Carbs 0 g
- Fiber 0 g
- Sugar 0 g
- Protein 31.6 g

Seasoned Tuna

Preparation Time: 5 minutes

Cooking Time: 6 minutes

Servings: 2

Ingredients:

- 2 (6-ounce) yellowfin tuna steaks
- 2 tablespoons blackening seasoning
- Olive oil cooking spray

Method:

1. Coat the tuna steaks with the blackening seasoning evenly.
2. Then spray tuna steaks with cooking spray.
3. Place the water tray in the bottom of Power XL Smokeless Electric Grill.
4. Place about 2 cups of lukewarm water into the water tray.
5. Place the drip pan over water tray and then arrange the heating element.
6. Now, place the grilling pan over heating element.
7. Plugin the Power XL Smokeless Electric Grill and press the 'Power' button to turn it on.
8. Then press 'Fan" button.
9. Set the temperature settings according to manufacturer's directions.
10. Cover the grill with lid and let it preheat.
11. After preheating, remove the lid and grease the grilling pan.
12. Place the tuna steaks over the grilling pan.
13. Cover with the lid and cook for about 2-3 minutes per side.
14. Serve hot.

Nutritional Information per Serving:

- Calories 313
- Total Fat 10.7 g
- Saturated Fat 2.2 g
- Cholesterol 83 mg
- Sodium 169 mg
- Total Carbs 0 g
- Fiber 0 g
- Sugar 0 g
- Protein 50.9 g

Buttered Halibut

Preparation Time: 5 minutes

Cooking Time: 8 minutes

Servings: 2

Ingredients:

- 2 (4-ounce) haddock fillets
- Salt and ground black pepper, as required
- 1 tablespoon butter, melted

Method:

1. Sprinkle the fish fillets with salt and black pepper generously.
2. Place the water tray in the bottom of Power XL Smokeless Electric Grill.
3. Place about 2 cups of lukewarm water into the water tray.
4. Place the drip pan over water tray and then arrange the heating element.
5. Now, place the grilling pan over heating element.
6. Plugin the Power XL Smokeless Electric Grill and press the 'Power' button to turn it on.
7. Then press 'Fan" button.
8. Set the temperature settings according to manufacturer's directions.
9. Cover the grill with lid and let it preheat.
10. After preheating, remove the lid and grease the grilling pan.
11. Place the fish fillets over the grilling pan.
12. Cover with the lid and cook for about 3-4 minutes per side.
13. Remove from the grill and place the haddock fillets onto serving plates.
14. Drizzle with melted butter and serve.

Nutritional Information per Serving:

- Calories 178
- Total Fat 6.8 g
- Saturated Fat 3.8 g
- Cholesterol 99 mg
- Sodium 217 mg
- Total Carbs 0 g
- Fiber 0 g
- Sugar 0 g
- Protein 27.6 g

Shrimp Kabobs

Preparation Time: 15 minutes

Cooking Time: 8 minutes

Servings: 6

Ingredients:

- 1 jalapeño pepper, chopped
- 1 large garlic clove, chopped
- 1 (1-inch) fresh ginger, mined
- 1/3 cup fresh mint leaves
- 1 cup coconut milk
- ¼ cup fresh lime juice
- 1 tablespoon red boat fish sauce
- 24 medium shrimp, peeled and deveined
- 1 avocado, peeled, pitted and cubed
- 3 cups seedless watermelon, cubed

Method:

1. In a food processor, add jalapeño, garlic, ginger, mint, coconut milk, lime juice and fish sauce and pulse until smooth.
2. Add shrimp and coat with marinade generously.
3. Cover and refrigerate to marinate for at least 1-2 hours.
4. Remove shrimp from marinade and thread onto pre-soaked wooden skewers with avocado and watermelon.
5. Place the water tray in the bottom of Power XL Smokeless Electric Grill.
6. Place about 2 cups of lukewarm water into the water tray.
7. Place the drip pan over water tray and then arrange the heating element.
8. Now, place the grilling pan over heating element.
9. Plugin the Power XL Smokeless Electric Grill and press the 'Power' button to turn it on.
10. Then press 'Fan" button.
11. Set the temperature settings according to manufacturer's directions.
12. Cover the grill with lid and let it preheat.

13. After preheating, remove the lid and grease the grilling pan.

14. Place the skewers over the grilling pan.

15. Cover with the lid and cook for about 3-4 minutes per side.

16. Serve hot.

Nutritional Information per Serving:

- Calories 294
- Total Fat 17.7 g
- Saturated Fat 10.4 g
- Cholesterol 185mg
- Sodium 473 mg
- Total Carbs 12.9 g
- Fiber 3.8 g
- Sugar 6.2 g
- Protein 22.9 g

CHAPTER 8: BURGERS RECIPES

Turkey Burgers

Preparation Time: 15 minutes

Cooking Time: 12 minutes

Servings: 4

Ingredients:

- Olive oil cooking spray
- 12 ounces lean ground turkey
- ½ of apple, peeled, cored and grated
- ½ of red bell pepper, seeded and chopped finely
- ¼ cup red onion, minced
- 2 small garlic cloves, minced
- 1 tablespoon fresh ginger, minced
- 2½ tablespoons fresh cilantro, chopped
- 2 tablespoons curry paste
- 1 teaspoon ground cumin
- 1 teaspoon olive oil

Method:

1. In a large bowl, add all the ingredients except for oil and mix until well combined.
2. Make 4 equal-sized burgers from mixture.
3. Brush the burgers with olive oil evenly.
4. Place the water tray in the bottom of Power XL Smokeless Electric Grill.
5. Place about 2 cups of lukewarm water into the water tray.
6. Place the drip pan over water tray and then arrange the heating element.
7. Now, place the grilling pan over heating element.
8. Plugin the Power XL Smokeless Electric Grill and press the 'Power' button to turn it on.
9. Then press 'Fan" button.
10. Set the temperature settings according to manufacturer's directions.

11. Cover the grill with lid and let it preheat.

12. After preheating, remove the lid and grease the grilling pan.

13. Place the <u>steak</u> over the grilling pan.

14. Cover with the lid and cook for about 5-6 minutes per side.

15. Serve hot.

Nutritional Information per Serving:

- Calories 258
- Total Fat 15.2 g
- Saturated Fat 1.8 g
- Cholesterol 87 mg
- Sodium 94 mg
- Total Carbs 9.5 g
- Fiber 1.3 g
- Sugar 4 g
- Protein 24.3 g

Lamb Burgers

Preparation Time: 15 minutes

Cooking Time: 16 minutes

Servings: 5

Ingredients:

- 2 pounds ground lamb
- 9 ounces Halloumi cheese, grated
- 2 eggs
- 1 tablespoon fresh rosemary, chopped finely
- 1 tablespoon fresh parsley, chopped finely
- 2 teaspoons ground cumin
- Salt and ground black pepper, as required

Method:

1. In a large bowl, add all the ingredients and mix until well combined.
2. Make 10 equal-sized patties from the mixture.
3. Place the water tray in the bottom of Power XL Smokeless Electric Grill.
4. Place about 2 cups of lukewarm water into the water tray.
5. Place the drip pan over water tray and then arrange the heating element.
6. Now, place the grilling pan over heating element.
7. Plugin the Power XL Smokeless Electric Grill and press the 'Power' button to turn it on.
8. Then press 'Fan" button.
9. Set the temperature settings according to manufacturer's directions.
10. Cover the grill with lid and let it preheat.
11. After preheating, remove the lid and grease the grilling pan.
12. Place the burgers over the grilling pan.
13. Cover with the lid and cook for about 15-8 minutes per side.
14. Serve hot

Nutritional Information per Serving:

- Calories 554
- Total Fat 30.6 g
- Saturated Fat 15.9 g
- Cholesterol 269 mg
- Sodium 459 mg
- Total Carbs 2.3 g
- Fiber 0.4 g
- Sugar 1.5 g
- Protein 64.4 g

Beef Burgers

Preparation Time: 15 minutes

Cooking Time: 8 minutes

Servings: 4

Ingredients:

- 1 pound lean ground beef
- ¼ cup fresh parsley, chopped
- ¼ cup fresh parsley, chopped
- ¼ cup fresh cilantro, chopped
- 1 tablespoon fresh ginger, chopped
- 1 teaspoon ground cumin
- 1 teaspoon ground coriander
- ½ teaspoon ground cinnamon
- Salt and ground black pepper, as required

Method:

1. In a bowl, add the beef, ¼ cup of parsley, cilantro, ginger, spices, salt and black pepper and mix until well combined.
2. Make 4 equal-sized patties from the mixture.
3. Place the water tray in the bottom of Power XL Smokeless Electric Grill.
4. Place about 2 cups of lukewarm water into the water tray.
5. Place the drip pan over water tray and then arrange the heating element.
6. Now, place the grilling pan over heating element.
7. Plugin the Power XL Smokeless Electric Grill and press the 'Power' button to turn it on.
8. Then press 'Fan" button.
9. Set the temperature settings according to manufacturer's directions.
10. Cover the grill with lid and let it preheat.
11. After preheating, remove the lid and grease the grilling pan.
12. Place the burgers over the grilling pan.
13. Cover with the lid and cook for about for about 3-4 minutes per side or until desired doneness.
14. Serve hot.

Nutritional Information per Serving:

- Calories 220
- Total Fat 7.3 g
- Saturated Fat 2.7 g
- Cholesterol 101 mg
- Sodium 117 mg
- Total Carbs 1.7 g
- Fiber 0.5 g
- Sugar 0.1 g
- Protein 34.8 g

Stuffed Burgers

Preparation Time: 15 minutes

Cooking Time: 20 minutes

Servings: 10

Ingredients:

For Filling:

- 2 cups cooked ham, chopped
- 2 cups fresh mushrooms, chopped
- 2 cups onion, chopped
- 3 cups cheddar cheese, shredded

For Patties:

- 5 pounds lean ground beef
- 1/3 cup Worcestershire sauce
- 2 teaspoons hickory seasoning
- Salt and ground black pepper, as required

Method:

1. For filling: in a bowl, mix together all ingredients. Set aside.
2. For patties: in another large bowl, add all ingredients and mix until well combined.
3. Divide beef mixture into 20 equal portions. Make equal sized patties from each portion.
4. Place 10 patties onto a smooth surface. Place cheese mixture over each patty evenly.
5. Cover with remaining patties, by pressing the edges to secure the filling.
6. Place the water tray in the bottom of Power XL Smokeless Electric Grill.
7. Place about 2 cups of lukewarm water into the water tray.
8. Place the drip pan over water tray and then arrange the heating element.
9. Now, place the grilling pan over heating element.
10. Plugin the Power XL Smokeless Electric Grill and press the 'Power' button to turn it on.
11. Then press 'Fan" button.
12. Set the temperature settings according to manufacturer's directions.
13. Cover the grill with lid and let it preheat.
14. After preheating, remove the lid and grease the grilling pan.

15. Place the burgers over the grilling pan.

16. Cover with the lid and cook for about 8-10 minutes per side.

17. Serve hot.

Nutritional Information per Serving:

- Calories 623
- Total Fat 27.7 g
- Saturated Fat 13.3 g
- Cholesterol 254 mg
- Sodium 865 mg
- Total Carbs 5.9 g
- Fiber 1 g
- Sugar 3.1 g
- Protein 82.4 g

Quinoa Burgers

Preparation Time: 20 minutes

Cooking Time: 10 minutes

Servings: 6

Ingredients:

For Burgers:

- 1 tablespoon extra-virgin olive oil
- ½ of red onion, chopped
- 1 garlic clove, minced
- 1 cup fresh kale, tough ribs removed
- 1 cup carrots, peeled and chopped roughly
- 1/3 cup fresh parsley
- 15 ounces cooked cannellini beans, drained and rinsed
- 1 cup cooked quinoa
- 1 cup gluten-free oats

For Seasoning Mixture:

- ½ cup barbecue sauce
- 1 teaspoon dried oregano
- 1 teaspoon chili powder
- 1 teaspoon ground cumin

Method:

1. For burgers: in a medium pan, heat the oil over medium heat and sauté the onion and garlic for about 5 minutes.
2. With a slotted spoon, transfer the onion mixture into the large bowl.
3. In a food processor, add kale, carrots and parsley and pulse until grated.
4. Transfer the kale mixture into the bowl of onion mixture.
5. In the food processor, add white beans to and pulse until mashed slightly.
6. Transfer the mashed beans into the bowl of kale mixture.
7. For seasoning mixture: in a small mixing bowl, add all ingredients and mix well.

8. Add the cooked quinoa, oats and seasoning mixture in the bowl of kale mixture and mix until well combined.

9. Make 6 equal-sized patties from the mixture.

10. Place the water tray in the bottom of Power XL Smokeless Electric Grill.

11. Place about 2 cups of lukewarm water into the water tray.

12. Place the drip pan over water tray and then arrange the heating element.

13. Now, place the grilling pan over heating element.

14. Plugin the Power XL Smokeless Electric Grill and press the 'Power' button to turn it on.

15. Then press 'Fan" button.

16. Set the temperature settings according to manufacturer's directions.

17. Cover the grill with lid and let it preheat.

18. After preheating, remove the lid and grease the grilling pan.

19. Place the burgers over the grilling pan.

20. Cover with the lid and cook for about 4-5 minutes per side.

21. Serve hot.

Nutritional Information per Serving:

- Calories 489
- Total Fat 6.4 g
- Saturated Fat 0.9 g
- Cholesterol 0 mg
- Sodium 276 mg
- Total Carbs 86.5 g
- Fiber 24 g
- Sugar 8.4 g
- Protein 24.1 g

CHAPTER 9: VEGETARIAN RECIPES

Basil Pizza

Preparation Time: 10 minutes

Cooking Time: 7 minutes

Servings: 2

Ingredients:

- 1 pizza dough
- ½ tablespoon olive oil
- 1 cup pizza sauce
- 1½ cups part-skim mozzarella cheese, shredded
- 1½ cups part-skim provolone cheese, shredded
- 10 fresh basil leaves

Method:

1. Place the water tray in the bottom of Power XL Smokeless Electric Grill.
2. Place about 2 cups of lukewarm water into the water tray.
3. Place the drip pan over water tray and then arrange the heating element.
4. Now, place the grilling pan over heating element.
5. Plugin the Power XL Smokeless Electric Grill and press the 'Power' button to turn it on.
6. Then press 'Fan" button.
7. Set the temperature settings according to manufacturer's directions.
8. Cover the grill with lid and let it preheat.
9. With your hands, stretch the dough into the size that will fit into the grilling pan.
10. After preheating, remove the lid and grease the grilling pan.
11. Place the dough over the grilling pan.
12. Cover with the lid and cook for about 2-3 minutes
13. Remove the lid and with a heat-safe spatula, flip the dough.
14. Cover with the lid and cook for about 2 minutes.
15. Remove the lid and flip the crust.

16. Immediately, spread the pizza sauce over the crust and sprinkle with both kinds of cheese.
17. Cover with the lid and cook for about 1 minute.
18. Remove the lid and cook for about 1 minute or until the cheese is melted.
19. Remove from the grill and immediately top the pizza with basil leaves.
20. Cut into desired sized wedges and serve.

Nutritional Information per Serving:

- Calories 707
- Total Fat 47.5 g
- Saturated Fat 23.1 g
- Cholesterol 80 mg
- Sodium 1000 mg
- Total Carbs 34.9 g
- Fiber 3.5 g
- Sugar 4.6 g
- Protein 35.8 g

Grilled Cauliflower

Preparation Time: 15 minutes

Cooking Time: 40 minutes

Servings: 4

Ingredients:

- 1 large head of cauliflower, leaves removed and stem trimmed
- Salt, as required
- 4 tablespoons unsalted butter
- ¼ cup hot sauce
- 1 tablespoon ketchup
- 1 tablespoon soy sauce
- ½ cup mayonnaise
- 2 tablespoons white miso
- 1 tablespoon fresh lemon juice
- ½ teaspoon ground black pepper
- 2 scallions, thinly sliced

Method:

1. Sprinkle the cauliflower with salt evenly.
2. Arrange the cauliflower head in a large microwave-safe bowl.
3. With a plastic wrap, cover the bowl.
4. With a knife, pierce the plastic a few times to vent.
5. Microwave on high for about 5 minutes.
6. Remove from the microwave and set aside to cool slightly.
7. In a small saucepan, add butter, hot sauce, ketchup and soy sauce over medium heat and cook for about 2-3 minutes, stirring occasionally.
8. Brush the cauliflower head with warm sauce evenly.
9. Place the water tray in the bottom of Power XL Smokeless Electric Grill.
10. Place about 2 cups of lukewarm water into the water tray.
11. Place the drip pan over water tray and then arrange the heating element.
12. Now, place the grilling pan over heating element.

13. Plugin the Power XL Smokeless Electric Grill and press the 'Power' button to turn it on.

14. Then press 'Fan" button.

15. Set the temperature settings according to manufacturer's directions.

16. Cover the grill with lid and let it preheat.

17. After preheating, remove the lid and grease the grilling pan.

18. Place the cauliflower head over the grilling pan.

19. Cover with the lid and cook for about 10 minutes.

20. Turn the cauliflower over and brush with warm sauce.

21. Cover with the lid and cook for about 25 minutes, flipping and brushing with warm sauce after every 10 minutes.

22. Transfer cauliflower to a plate and let cool slightly.

23. In a bowl, place the mayonnaise, miso, lemon juice, and pepper and beat until smooth.

24. Spread the mayonnaise mixture onto a plate and arrange the cauliflower on top.

25. Garnish with scallions and serve.

Nutritional Information per Serving:

- Calories 261
- Total Fat 22 g
- Saturated Fat 8.9 g
- Cholesterol 38 mg
- Sodium 1300mg
- Total Carbs 15.1 g
- Fiber 2.5 g
- Sugar 5.4 g
- Protein 3.3 g

Stuffed Zucchini

Preparation Time: 20 minutes

Cooking Time: 24 minutes

Servings: 6

Ingredients:

- 3 medium zucchinis, sliced in half lengthwise
- 1 teaspoon vegetable oil
- Salt and ground black pepper, as required
- 3 cup corn, cut off the cob
- 1 cup Parmesan cheese, shredded
- 2/3 cup sour cream
- ¼ teaspoon hot sauce
- Olive oil cooking spray

Method:

1. Cut the ends off the zucchini and slice in half lengthwise.
2. Scoop out the pulp from each half of zucchini, leaving the shell.
3. For filling: in a large pan of boiling water, add the corn over medium heat andcook for about 5-7 minutes.
4. Drain the corn and set aside to cool.
5. In a large bowl, add corn, haf of the parmesan cheese, sour cream and hot sauce and mix well.
6. Spray the zucchini shells with cooking spray evenly.
7. Place the water tray in the bottom of Power XL Smokeless Electric Grill.
8. Place about 2 cups of lukewarm water into the water tray.
9. Place the drip pan over water tray and then arrange the heating element.
10. Now, place the grilling pan over heating element.
11. Plugin the Power XL Smokeless Electric Grill and press the 'Power' button to turn it on.
12. Then press 'Fan" button.
13. Set the temperature settings according to manufacturer's directions.
14. Cover the grill with lid and let it preheat.
15. After preheating, remove the lid and grease the grilling pan.

16. Place the zucchini halves over the grilling pan, flesh side down.

17. Cover with the lid and cook for about 8-10 minutes.

18. Remove the zucchini halves from grill.

19. Spoon filling into each zucchini half evenly and sprinkle with remaining parmesan cheese.

20. Place the zucchini halves over the grilling pan.

21. Cover with the lid and cook for about 8 minutes.

22. Serve hot.

Nutritional Information per Serving:

- Calories 198
- Total Fat 10.8 g
- Saturated Fat 6 g
- Cholesterol 21 mg
- Sodium 293 mg
- Total Carbs 19.3 g
- Fiber 3.2 g
- Sugar 4.2 g
- Protein 9.6 g

Vinegar Veggies

Preparation Time: 15 minutes

Cooking Time: 10 minutes

Servings: 4

Ingredients:

- 3 golden beets, trimmed, peeled and sliced thinly
- 3 carrots, peeled and sliced lengthwise
- 1 cup zucchini, sliced
- 1 onion, sliced
- ½ cup yam, sliced thinly
- 2 tablespoon fresh rosemary
- 1 garlic clove, minced
- Salt and ground black pepper, as required
- 3 tablespoons vegetable oil
- 2 teaspoons balsamic vinegar

Method:

1. Place all ingredients in a bowl and toss to coat well.
2. Refrigerate to marinate for at least 30 minutes.
3. Place the water tray in the bottom of Power XL Smokeless Electric Grill.
4. Place about 2 cups of lukewarm water into the water tray.
5. Place the drip pan over water tray and then arrange the heating element.
6. Now, place the grilling pan over heating element.
7. Plugin the Power XL Smokeless Electric Grill and press the 'Power' button to turn it on.
8. Then press 'Fan" button.
9. Set the temperature settings according to manufacturer's directions.
10. Cover the grill with lid and let it preheat.
11. After preheating, remove the lid and grease the grilling pan.
12. Place the vegetables over the grilling pan.
13. Cover with the lid and cook for about 5 minutes per side.
14. Serve hot.

Nutritional Information per Serving:

- Calories 184
- Total Fat 10.7 g
- Saturated Fat 2.2 g
- Cholesterol 0 mg
- Sodium 134 mg
- Total Carbs 21.5 g
- Fiber 4.9 g
- Sugar 10 g
- Protein 2.7 g

Garlicky Mixed Veggies

Preparation Time: 15 minutes

Cooking Time: 8 minutes

Servings: 4

Ingredients:

- 1 bunch fresh asparagus, trimmed
- 6 ounces fresh mushrooms, halved
- 6 Campari tomatoes, halved
- 1 red onion, cut into 1-inch chunks
- 3 garlic cloves, minced
- 2 tablespoons olive oil
- Salt and ground black pepper, as required

Method:

1. In a large bowl, add all ingredients and toss to coat well.
2. Place the water tray in the bottom of Power XL Smokeless Electric Grill.
3. Place about 2 cups of lukewarm water into the water tray.
4. Place the drip pan over water tray and then arrange the heating element.
5. Now, place the grilling pan over heating element.
6. Plugin the Power XL Smokeless Electric Grill and press the 'Power' button to turn it on.
7. Then press 'Fan" button.
8. Set the temperature settings according to manufacturer's directions.
9. Cover the grill with lid and let it preheat.
10. After preheating, remove the lid and grease the grilling pan.
11. Place the vegetables over the grilling pan.
12. Cover with the lid and cook for about 8 minutes, flipping occasionally.

Nutritional Information per Serving:

- Calories 137
- Total Fat 7.7 g
- Saturated Fat 1.1 g
- Cholesterol 0 mg
- Sodium 54 mg
- Total Carbs 15.6 g
- Fiber 5.6 g
- Sugar 8.9 g
- Protein 5.8 g

Mediterranean Veggies

Preparation Time: 5 minutes

Cooking Time: 10 minutes

Servings: 4

Ingredients:

- 1 cup mixed bell peppers, chopped
- 1 cup eggplant, chopped
- 1 cup zucchini, chopped
- 1 cup mushrooms, chopped
- ½ cup onion, chopped
- ½ cup sun-dried tomato vinaigrette dressing

Method:

1. In a large bowl, add all ingredients and toss to coat well.
2. Refrigerate to marinate for about 1 hour.
3. Place the water tray in the bottom of Power XL Smokeless Electric Grill.
4. Place about 2 cups of lukewarm water into the water tray.
5. Place the drip pan over water tray and then arrange the heating element.
6. Now, place the grilling pan over heating element.
7. Plugin the Power XL Smokeless Electric Grill and press the 'Power' button to turn it on.
8. Then press 'Fan" button.
9. Set the temperature settings according to manufacturer's directions.
10. Cover the grill with lid and let it preheat.
11. After preheating, remove the lid and grease the grilling pan.
12. Place the vegetables over the grilling pan.
13. Cover with the lid and cook for about 8-10 minutes, flipping occasionally.
14. Serve hot.

Nutritional Information per Serving:

- Calories 159
- Total Fat 11.2 g
- Saturated Fat 2 g
- Cholesterol 0 mg
- Sodium 336 mg
- Total Carbs 12.3 g
- Fiber 1.9 g
- Sugar 9.5 g
- Protein 1.6 g

Marinated Veggie Skewers

Preparation Time: 20 minutes

Cooking Time: 10 minutes

Servings: 4

Ingredients:

For Marinade:

- 2 garlic cloves, minced
- 2 teaspoons fresh basil, minced
- 2 teaspoons fresh oregano, minced
- ½ teaspoon cayenne pepper
- Sea Salt and ground black pepper, as required
- 2 tablespoons fresh lemon juice
- 2 tablespoons olive oil

For Veggies:

- 2 large zucchinis, cut into thick slices
- 8 large button mushrooms, quartered
- 1 yellow bell pepper, seeded and cubed
- 1 red bell pepper, seeded and cubed

Method:

1. For marinade: in a large bowl, add all the ingredients and mix until well combined.
2. Add the vegetables and toss to coat well.
3. Cover and refrigerate to marinate for at least 6-8 hours.
4. Remove the vegetables from the bowl and thread onto pre-soaked wooden skewers.
5. Place the water tray in the bottom of Power XL Smokeless Electric Grill.
6. Place about 2 cups of lukewarm water into the water tray.
7. Place the drip pan over water tray and then arrange the heating element.
8. Now, place the grilling pan over heating element.
9. Plugin the Power XL Smokeless Electric Grill and press the 'Power' button to turn it on.
10. Then press 'Fan" button.
11. Set the temperature settings according to manufacturer's directions.

12. Cover the grill with lid and let it preheat.

13. After preheating, remove the lid and grease the grilling pan.

14. Place the skewers over the grilling pan.

15. Cover with the lid and cook for about 8-10 minutes, flipping occasionally.

16. Serve hot.

Nutritional Information per Serving:

- Calories 122
- Total Fat 7.8 g
- Saturated Fat 1.2 g
- Cholesterol 0 mg
- Sodium 81 mg
- Total Carbs 12.7 g
- Fiber 3.5 g
- Sugar 6.8g
- Protein 4.3 g

Pineapple & Veggie Skewers

Preparation Time: 20 minutes

Cooking Time: 15 minutes

Servings: 6

Ingredients:

- 1/3 cup olive oil
- 1½ teaspoons dried basil
- ¾ teaspoon dried oregano
- Salt and ground black pepper, as required
- 2 zucchinis, cut into 1-inch slices
- 2 yellow squash, cut into 1-inch slices
- ½ pound whole fresh mushrooms
- 1 red bell pepper, cut into chunks
- 1 red onion, cut into chunks
- 12 cherry tomatoes
- 1 fresh pineapple, cut into chunks

Method:

1. In a bowl, add oil, herbs, salt ad black pepper and mix well.
2. Thread the veggies and pineapple onto pre-soaked wooden skewers.
3. Brush the veggiesand pineapple with oil mixture evenly.
4. Place the water tray in the bottom of Power XL Smokeless Electric Grill.
5. Place about 2 cups of lukewarm water into the water tray.
6. Place the drip pan over water tray and then arrange the heating element.
7. Now, place the grilling pan over heating element.
8. Plugin the Power XL Smokeless Electric Grill and press the 'Power' button to turn it on.
9. Then press 'Fan" button.
10. Set the temperature settings according to manufacturer's directions.
11. Cover the grill with lid and let it preheat.
12. After preheating, remove the lid and grease the grilling pan.
13. Place the skewers over the grilling pan.

4. Cover with the lid and cook for about 10-15 minutes, flipping occasionally.

5. Serve hot.

Nutritional Information per Serving:

Calories 220

Total Fat 11.9 g

- Saturated Fat 1.7 g

- Cholesterol 0 mg

- Sodium 47 mg

- Total Carbs 30 g

- Fiber 5 g

- Sugar 20.4 g

- Protein 4.3 g

Buttered Corn

Preparation Time: 10 minutes

Cooking Time: 20 minutes

Servings: 6

Ingredients:

- 6 fresh whole corn on the cob
- ½ cup butter, melted
- Salt, as required

Method:

1. Husk the corn and remove all the silk.
2. Brush each corn with melted butter and sprinkle with salt.
3. Place the water tray in the bottom of Power XL Smokeless Electric Grill.
4. Place about 2 cups of lukewarm water into the water tray.
5. Place the drip pan over water tray and then arrange the heating element.
6. Now, place the grilling pan over heating element.
7. Plugin the Power XL Smokeless Electric Grill and press the 'Power' button to turn it on.
8. Then press 'Fan" button.
9. Set the temperature settings according to manufacturer's directions.
10. Cover the grill with lid and let it preheat.
11. After preheating, remove the lid and grease the grilling pan.
12. Place the corn over the grilling pan.
13. Cover with the lid and cook for about 20 minutes, rotating after every 5 minutes and brushing with butter once halfway through.
14. Serve warm.

Nutritional Information per Serving:

- Calories 268
- Total Fat 17.2 g
- Saturated Fat 10 g
- Cholesterol 41 mg
- Sodium 159 mg
- Total Carbs 29 g
- Fiber 4.2 g
- Sugar 5 g
- Protein 5.2 g

Guacamole

Preparation Time: 15 minutes

Cooking Time: 4 minutes

Servings: 4

Ingredients:

- 2 ripe avocados, halved and pitted
- 2 teaspoons vegetable oil
- 3 tablespoons fresh lime juice
- 1 garlic clove, crushed
- ¼ teaspoon ground chipotle chile
- Salt, as required
- ¼ cup red onion, chopped finely
- ¼ cup fresh cilantro, chopped finely

Method:

1. Brush the cut sides of each avocado half with oil.
2. Place the water tray in the bottom of Power XL Smokeless Electric Grill.
3. Place about 2 cups of lukewarm water into the water tray.
4. Place the drip pan over water tray and then arrange the heating element.
5. Now, place the grilling pan over heating element.
6. Plugin the Power XL Smokeless Electric Grill and press the 'Power' button to turn it on.
7. Then press 'Fan" button.
8. Set the temperature settings according to manufacturer's directions.
9. Cover the grill with lid and let it preheat.
10. After preheating, remove the lid and grease the grilling pan.
11. Place the avocado halves over the grilling pan, cut side down.
12. Cook, uncovered for about 2-4 minutes.
13. Transfer the avocados onto cutting board and let them cool slightly.
14. Remove the peel and transfer the flesh into a bowl.
15. Add the lime juice, garlic, chipotle and salt and with a fork, mash until almost smooth.
16. Stir in onion and cilantro and refrigerate, covered for about 1 hour before serving.

Nutritional Information per Serving:

- Calories 230
- Total Fat 21.9 g
- Saturated Fat 4.6g
- Cholesterol 0 mg
- Sodium 46 mg
- Total Carbs 9.7 g
- Fiber 6.9 g
- Sugar 0.8 g
- Protein 2.1 g

CHAPTER 10: DESSERT RECIPES

Grilled Peaches

Preparation Time: 10 minutes

Cooking Time: 4 minutes

Servings: 4

Ingredients:

- 4 ripe peaches, halved and pitted
- 2 tablespoons maple syrup

Method:

1. Place the water tray in the bottom of Power XL Smokeless Electric Grill.
2. Place about 2 cups of lukewarm water into the water tray.
3. Place the drip pan over water tray and then arrange the heating element.
4. Now, place the grilling pan over heating element.
5. Plugin the Power XL Smokeless Electric Grill and press the 'Power' button to turn it on.
6. Then press 'Fan" button.
7. Set the temperature settings according to manufacturer's directions.
8. Cover the grill with lid and let it preheat.
9. After preheating, remove the lid and grease the grilling pan.
10. Place the peach halves over the grilling pan, flesh side down.
11. Cover with the lid and cook for about 3-4 minutes.
12. Drizzle with maple syrup and serve.

Nutritional Information per Serving:

- Calories 110
- Total Fat 0.4 g
- Saturated Fat 0 g
- Cholesterol 0 mg
- Sodium 2 mg
- Total Carbs 27.2 g
- Fiber 2.3 g
- Sugar 25.7 g
- Protein 1.4 g

Nectarine

Preparation Time: 10 minutes

Cooking Time: 6 minutes

Servings: 2

Ingredients:

- 2 medium nectarines, halved and pitted
- 1 tablespoon butter, melted
- 2 tablespoons honey
- ½ teaspoon ground nutmeg

Method:

1. Brush the nectarine halves with butter evenly.
2. Place the water tray in the bottom of Power XL Smokeless Electric Grill.
3. Place about 2 cups of lukewarm water into the water tray.
4. Place the drip pan over water tray and then arrange the heating element.
5. Now, place the grilling pan over heating element.
6. Plugin the Power XL Smokeless Electric Grill and press the 'Power' button to turn it on.
7. Then press 'Fan" button.
8. Set the temperature settings according to manufacturer's directions.
9. Cover the grill with lid and let it preheat.
10. After preheating, remove the lid and grease the grilling pan.
11. Place the nectarine halves over the grilling pan.
12. Cook, uncovered for about 5-6 minutes, flipping and brushing with honey occasionally.
13. Transfer the nectarine halves onto a platter and set aside to cool.
14. Sprinkle with nutmeg and serve.

Nutritional Information per Serving:

- Calories 180
- Total Fat 6.4 g
- Saturated Fat 3.8 g
- Cholesterol 15 mg
- Sodium 42 mg
- Total Carbs 32.6 g
- Fiber 2.6 g
- Sugar 28.6 g
- Protein 1.7 g

Sugared Bananas

Preparation Time: 10 minutes

Cooking Time: 5 minutes

Servings: 6

Ingredients:

- 1¼ cups brown sugar
- 2 teaspoons ground cinnamon
- 6 unpeeled bananas, halved lengthwise
- 2 tablespoons fresh lemon juice

Method:

1. Place the brown sugar and cinnamon in a bowl and mix.
2. Drizzle the exposed surface of each banana half with lemon juice and then sprinkle with sugar mixture.
3. Place the water tray in the bottom of Power XL Smokeless Electric Grill.
4. Place about 2 cups of lukewarm water into the water tray.
5. Place the drip pan over water tray and then arrange the heating element.
6. Now, place the grilling pan over heating element.
7. Plugin the Power XL Smokeless Electric Grill and press the 'Power' button to turn it on.
8. Then press 'Fan" button.
9. Set the temperature settings according to manufacturer's directions.
10. Cover the grill with lid and let it preheat.
11. After preheating, remove the lid and grease the grilling pan.
12. Place banana halves over the grilling pan, peel side up
13. Cover with the lid and cook for about 2-3 minutes per side.
14. Transfer the banana halves bananas onto serving plates.
15. Remove the peel and serve.

Nutritional Information per Serving:

- Calories 223
- Total Fat 0.4 g
- Saturated Fat 0.2 g
- Cholesterol 0 mg
- Sodium 11 mg
- Total Carbs 57.3 g
- Fiber 3.5 g
- Sugar 43.9 g
- Protein 1.4 g

Pineapple

Preparation Time: 15 minutes

Cooking Time: 10 minutes

Servings: 6

Ingredients:

- ¾ cup tequila
- ¾ cup brown sugar
- 1½ teaspoons vanilla extract
- ½ teaspoon ground cinnamon
- 1 large pineapple, peeled, cored and cut into 1-inch-thick slices

Method:

1. Place tequila, sugar, vanilla and cinnamon in a bowl and mix well.
2. Place the water tray in the bottom of Power XL Smokeless Electric Grill.
3. Place about 2 cups of lukewarm water into the water tray.
4. Place the drip pan over water tray and then arrange the heating element.
5. Now, place the grilling pan over heating element.
6. Plugin the Power XL Smokeless Electric Grill and press the 'Power' button to turn it on.
7. Then press 'Fan" button.
8. Set the temperature settings according to manufacturer's directions.
9. Cover the grill with lid and let it preheat.
10. After preheating, remove the lid and grease the grilling pan.
11. Place the pineapple slices over the grilling pan.
12. Cover with the lid and cook for about 10 minutes, flipping and basting with tequila mixture occasionally.
13. Serve hot.

Nutritional Information per Serving:

- Calories 225
- Total Fat 0.2 g
- Saturated Fat 0 g
- Cholesterol 0 mg
- Sodium 8 mg
- Total Carbs 38.3 g
- Fiber 2.2 g
- Sugar 33 g
- Protein 0.8 g

Grilled Fruit Kabobs

Preparation Time: 15 minutes

Cooking Time: 10 minutes

Servings: 6

Ingredients:

- 1 cup pineapple, cut into 1-inch pieces
- 1 banana, cut into 1-inch pieces
- 1 cup cantaloupe, cut into 1-inch pieces
- 1 cup fresh strawberries, hulled
- Coconut oil cooking spray
- 1 tablespoon maple syrup

Method:

1. Thread the fruit pieces alternately onto pre-soaked wooden skewers.
2. Spray with cooking spray and then drizzle with maple syrup.
3. Place the water tray in the bottom of Power XL Smokeless Electric Grill.
4. Place about 2 cups of lukewarm water into the water tray.
5. Place the drip pan over water tray and then arrange the heating element.
6. Now, place the grilling pan over heating element.
7. Plugin the Power XL Smokeless Electric Grill and press the 'Power' button to turn it on.
8. Then press 'Fan" button.
9. Set the temperature settings according to manufacturer's directions.
10. Cover the grill with lid and let it preheat.
11. After preheating, remove the lid and grease the grilling pan.
12. Place the skewers over the grilling pan.
13. Cover with the lid and cook for about 10 minutes, flipping occasionally.
14. Serve immediately.

Nutritional Information per Serving:

- Calories 56
- Total Fat 0.2 g
- Saturated Fat 0 g
- Cholesterol 0 mg
- Sodium 5 mg
- Total Carbs 14.3 g
- Fiber 1.6 g
- Sugar 10.3 g
- Protein 0.7 g

CPSIA information can be obtained
at www.ICGtesting.com
Printed in the USA
BVHW051942020122
625321BV00012B/861